"I have known Jana Hoffman for almost tell you: Jana is a warrior in prayer. For y̲ ̲̲ ̲̲ ̲̲ ̲̲ ̲̲ ̲̲ ̲̲ ̲̲ ̲̲ ̲̲ ̲̲ ̲̲ ̲̲ by and learned from her ministry of prayer. I commend this book to you as a helpful guide, manual, and tool for exploring how to deepen the work and privilege of prayer. May God use it to bless His people! I know it will bless you."

—**Kyle Worley,**
*Knowing Faith* Podcast Host,
Pastor, Mosaic Church, Richardson, Texas

"Jana Hoffman is a woman of prayer who seeks the Lord with a heart full of deep love and passion to see other women seek the Lord through prayer. My wife, Esther, and I were privileged to have Jana share her testimony and practically exemplify her prayer life when she spoke and encouraged women and families during Trauma Counseling for Women at Rift Valley Hope Ministries in Kenya, East Africa, in 2018 and 2019. I was moved and challenged as I witnessed the Holy Spirit lead her tender heart to pray with and comfort many of these women whose hearts are broken but are recovering and healing from their past traumas at our Rift Valley Hope.

"Reading Jana's book will encourage and move your heart deeply into seeking a consistent and continued prayer conversation with God that will no doubt lead your heart to yearn for a deeper love not only for our loving God but also for people of all backgrounds and nations created in the image of God. God desires to be more present in those people's lives through a deeper and more prayerful life relationship.

"I pray that the scriptures and reflections in this book will move and encourage us to seek to incline our hearts more to the heart and presence of God daily through prayer conversations and scripture."

—**Isaac K. Munji,**
Pastor, Professional Christian Counselor,
Spiritual Care Professional with ACPE, Inc.
(Association of Clinical Pastoral Education), Founder and Executive
Director of Rift Valley Hope Ministries, Kenya, East Africa

"My wife, Cindy, and I have valued our friendship with Jana and Mark Hoffman for more than 30 years. We have enjoyed many times of treasured fellowship, reviving worship, spiritual refreshment, nurturing Bible study, and missional outreach. Jana's deep love for the Lord, her pure joy in worshipping Jesus, and her deep passion for enriching prayer define her own intimacy with God. With the book you are now holding, you will get to know Jana's heart for the Lord as she shares her manifesto of faith and discipleship."

**—Dick Read,**
Pastor of Discipleship,
Asbury UMC, Tulsa, Oklahoma

"I am thrilled to be able to recommend Jana Hoffman's book, *Intimacy with God*. This is a book written from a precious soul who is given to intimacy with God. Jana and her husband, Mark, have co-labored with us for more than a decade in ministry and work of prayer, and I have seen them live this book out in real life. Jana says in her Introduction, 'Jesus loves you so, and he desires to spend time with you.' That is why I am so grateful for this book so that you can gain a deeper understanding of the Father's love for you. May the Lord use this study to help you experience what Jesus prayed for you in John 17:26."

**—Steve Hardin,**
Lead Campus Pastor,
White Rock Campus of Lake Pointe Church

"Jana Hoffman is a deep well of wisdom when it comes to understanding what it means for Christians to be truly surrendered to and led by the Holy Spirit. In this book, Jana gives the reader practical ways to open themselves up to the guidance of the Holy Spirit in their everyday lives. Jana shares rich gems of her own experiences with the Holy Spirit that give the reader a glimpse into the intimate adventure that awaits the Christian. This book will encourage your soul and leave you longing for more awareness of the Holy Spirit at work in your own life. What a gift we have been given from Jana Hoffman—a book that shows us how to take hold of the treasure that is found through life with the Holy Spirit of God. You will surely be blessed!"

**—Krystle Gutierrez,**
TV News Anchor and Reporter


"It has been a true joy to see Jana's love and giftedness in prayer over the years. In *Intimacy with God*, Jana guides the reader through scriptures on prayer, the prayer lives of biblical characters, the names of God, and more to give an understanding of the necessity and privilege of prayer. Whether you are new in your relationship with Jesus Christ or he has been the Lord of your life for decades, this book serves as an incredible guide to communing with God in deep, meaningful ways that will no doubt shape you through prayer into the image of Christ."

**—Rachel Joy,**
Founder and Executive Director,
Sparrow Collective, Lewisville, Texas

# Intimacy with God

### EVERLASTING CONVERSATIONS
### IN ALL OCCASIONS

*Jana Hoffman*

CLAY BRIDGES
PRESS

**Intimacy with God**

Everlasting Conversations in All Occasions

Copyright © 2020 by Jana Hoffman

Published by Clay Bridges in Houston, TX
www.ClayBridgesPress.com

Scripture quotations are taken from the Holy Bible, New International Version®, NIV®. Copyright © 1973, 1978, 1984, 2011 by Biblica, Inc.™ Used by permission of Zondervan. All rights reserved worldwide. www.zondervan.com The "NIV" and "New International Version" are trademarks registered in the United States Patent and Trademark Office by Biblica, Inc.™

ISBN: 978-1-953300-07-2
eISBN: 978-1-953300-09-6

Special Sales: Clay Bridges titles are available in wholesale quantity. Please visit www.claybridgesbulk.com to order 10 or more copies at a retail discount. Custom imprinting or excerpting can also be done to fit special needs. Contact Clay Bridges at Info@ClayBridgesPress.com.

# Dedication to the Ones I Love

This book is dedicated to all generations of my family whom I love and thank God for in my prayers. I was taught truth, integrity, hope, and love. I witnessed a praying family as the source in which to talk to God and wait to hear his voice. I'm growing in my ability to be forgiving like Christ, and daily I am being schooled by the many mysteries in the Bible.

Thank you to my husband, Mark, who loves me like Christ loved the church and gave himself up for her. You serve me so well. Daniel, Haven, Brandon, and Remington, you have been gracious, kind, and very patient with JaJa. I love our adventures together as a family.

Mark, you support me in every endeavor I run after. God knit us together as one. I love you.

Daniel, your wisdom is truly a beautiful gift from the Lord to behold. You continue to exercise patience, kindness, and a listening heart to comfort those in need.

Haven, your gift of joy, laughter, and a heart for prayer fills me with thankfulness.

Brandon, you are calm in times of trouble, and this reminds me to trust God even in trying times.

Remington, sweet baby—due to your pure heart, I experience Christ every time I am with you.

Oh, how I have loved praying with all of you for the past several years.

These stories have been knitted into the fabric of my life and nestled into my heart. Our life's scroll has been designed to give God all the glory and honor as it is written and read by others. Not just here on earth but for all eternity, our character matters. Truly, our stories are designed with purpose by the King, no matter the cost. Ultimately, the events that God allows us to journey through shape us to be more like Christ. His truth *is* our story.

# Table of Contents

# Foreword

## Mark Hoffman

It has been said there are three ways to read a book:

1.  Read the pictures.
2.  Read the words.
3.  Read the story.

There are also those who say to read a book one of these three ways:

1.  To glean whatever it has to offer you on the surface
2.  From the author's stated perspective or objective
3.  To discover deeper meanings (intended and unintended)

Well, I am about to offer you the distinct possibility that there is another way to read a book—particularly this book. Since this is a book about prayer, please consider asking the Holy Spirit to show you when is a good time to pause your reading and pray what you have just read. You can actually pray this book. I am particularly interested in those times when you are encouraged in your spirit to pray scripture back to God. Praying God's words and his will back to him is a good idea—especially if you are in a posture akin to what was present in the life of David, the writer of some of the Psalms.

So please use this prayer guide as a time to pray and soak up the full meaning of what is being communicated to you in scripture. The longer you linger with the words of the living God, the more you see and hear and feel and experience. These moments can change you and shape your character into the "more" that God has for you here on earth and beyond.

A sagacious young reporter once said, "We print what we can and what we have space for, but remember, there is always more to the story." There *is* always more to the story, and you are hopefully going to be part of that more. Hence, please tell us in writing at jana.hoffman@mac.com about what has happened in your life of prayer. We long to hear about your stories that bubble up as you read and remember and contemplate this book's purpose—a purpose that is expressed in the way God has spoken to you in your spirit as you have had your spirit speaking to its Maker in prayer. Dive headlong and heartfelt into prayer, and let us know when a moment of discernment happens, when you most fully grasp that God is God and you are not.

When you send us your stories and your experiences, we will include them (with your permission) in "The Rest of the Story" section after Jana's last chapter. You see, we want this book to be a living testament to God's pursuit of us as we live out our lives bathed in his living Word through prayer.

I have a friend whose wife never decides whether she will read a book from the beginning until she has read the ending to see if she likes it. Perhaps there are those of you who will enjoy checking out the stories from readers before you dive into this book. Who knows?

Agape and good reading and honest praying!

—Mark A. Hoffman, husband to Jana

# Rachael Rosser

The Lord instructs us to rejoice always, pray without ceasing, and give thanks in all circumstances. He reminds us that this is his will for all people.

I first met Jana Hoffman 10 years ago. Her name had been brought up many times as a godly woman I must meet. When we were finally introduced, I understood why. To know Jana is to get a glimpse of Jesus's heart. She is a woman who is gentle and lowly in her conversations and counsel with others. She listens intently, and I see her take to prayer after her conversations with others. Jana is obedient to follow what Paul exhorts us to do in Thessalonians. I have seen Jana minister to students, single and married women in Dallas, abused women in Zambia, and trafficked women in Kenya. In all those varied situations, I have seen her pray with and for these souls. I see her constantly not trying to fix people but to intercede for and with them. Her heart is tender toward her eternal Father and what he loves. She has spent much time at his feet both in his Word and in communicating with him. She has taught many how to have deeper intimacy with God by talking to him.

In 2 Chronicles 20, a great multitude came against Jehoshaphat and his kingdom. Jehoshaphat was afraid, and he set himself and asked the kingdom of Judah to seek the Lord through fasting and prayer. He was setting the example for his nation to follow by drawing closer to the heart of God in total dependence on him. Jehoshaphat then led the assembly in prayer, remembering and reminding God of his great power over all nations and heaven, his great works on behalf of his people, the past prayers cried out to God, the past obedience of his people, and God's promises to them. He finished leading the assembly by humbly confessing as the king that he did not have the answer to what was coming against them but that the only answer was to trust in God and look to him for their deliverance.

In a time when our world is in peril and unsure of what the next day holds, when world leaders contradict each other and information changes daily, our security is not in jeopardy. Even when we do not know what to do in response to crisis, we are reminded over and over to turn to God in prayer. I am grateful that Jana's book gives you steps to talk to our Father and to grow in your intimacy with him. My prayer for you is that as you read, you will go to God and find deeper intimacy and security through your conversations with him. He is the only firm foundation in shifting times.

In Jesus's name,
—Rachael Rosser, LPC Supervisor, Restore Biblical Counseling

# *Introduction*

*Intimacy with God brings affirmation of who you truly are in him. When we pray—God is with us—God is always with us.*

—Jana Hoffman

*I love those who love me, and those who seek me find me.*

—Prov. 8:17

*For the eyes of the Lord are on the righteous and his ears are attentive to their prayer.*

—1 Pet. 3:12

*He has made everything beautiful in its time. He has also set eternity in the human heart; yet no one can fathom what God has done from beginning to end.*

—Eccles. 3:11

*From one man he made all the nations, that they should inhabit the whole earth; and he marked out their appointed times in history and the boundaries of their lands. God did this so that they would seek him and perhaps reach out for him and find him, though he is not far from any one of us. "For in him we live and move and have our being." As some of your own poets have said, "We are his offspring."*

—Acts 17:26–28

Jesus is our greatest example on the subject of prayer. He was always looking to the Father for guidance: "Very truly I tell you, the Son can do nothing by himself; he can do only what He sees His Father doing" (John 5:19).

*So they took away the stone. Then Jesus looked up and said, "Father, I thank you that you have heard me. I knew that you always hear me, but I said this for the benefit of the people standing here, that they may believe that you sent me."*

—John 11:41–42

My earnest prayer is that as you read and pray this book, you will be in constant conversation with God, asking the Holy Spirit to guide you in all truth. My hope is that this book about spiritual intimacy will serve as a way for you to pause and study the passages during the section study guides. My heart is that you will be encouraged by the stories of his evidence. May your soul and spirit be greatly enlarged as you come to know Christ in a deeper and more passionate way through scripture, stories, prayer, and the power of the Holy Spirit. Jesus loves you so, and he desires to spend time with you.

Come, Holy Spirit, come.

Prayer changes us so we can more often change things in our lives and in the lives of those around us, and so we can finish this life strong.

We pray in order to become changed people to want and have more of God.

The scriptures below reveal that we are made in God's image. He has designed us and desires to hear his children talk with him. God longs for us to be near him as he is always with us, pursuing us, and loving us. (All the scripture throughout this book is from the New International Version.)

Joshua 1:9, Isaiah 41:10, Deuteronomy 31:6, Matthew 28:20, Hebrews 13:5, Romans 8:38–39, Zephaniah 3:17, Psalm 23:4, Matthew 25:34, 1 Corinthians 3:16, Revelation 3:20, John 14:16–17, Matthew 1:23, Ephesians 3:17, Psalm 46:1, Psalm 139:7–10, John 3:16, Psalm 23:1–6, Romans 5:8, 1 Peter 5:6–7, 2 Timothy 1:17, Isaiah 7:14, 1 John 1:9, John 14:23, Deuteronomy 31:8, John 1:14, Joshua 1:5–6, Jeremiah 23:23–24.

Jesus is the lifeline of preservation for our lives throughout all eternity with God. You might be wondering what it means to be intimate with God. The real question or thought is this: Do you know him?

Here is the beauty of this Holy God. God loves you. He created you in his image. It's called the Imago Dei. He is the master builder of who you are inside and out. You and I have sinful hearts. We walk in selfishness and in the pride of our flesh. We want our own way in everything we do, even if it is not good for our souls.

Jesus walked on this earth in order to bring forth the truth of why we were made like God. Jesus came to connect us to God's loving heart, and that's accomplished through the Holy Spirit. It was with joy and obedience that Christ went to the cross of death, even though he didn't have a selfish heart or a single sin in his life. Jesus was wrongfully put to death by crucifixion on a rustic wooden cross, which is the cruelest torture ever known to humanity throughout all of history. Jesus died. He rose to life on the third day, fulfilling scriptural prophecy from the Bible. He is the only deity in any religion whose grave is empty. He is with God now, yet he is going to return to gather the church, his bride, soon. We must be ready . . . set . . . go. Jesus is with God now, prevailing in prayer for you. He wants to give you life for all eternity, forever and ever, and his leaving brought the permanence of the Holy Spirit for your life and mine.

Beloved Cabin, Frisco, Colorado

He gives you an amazing gift of his Holy Spirit when you believe in him and ask him into your life. God will fill you with pure (not mixed or adulterated with any other substance or material) intimacy with his holy ways.

Dear Lord,

You are holy, good, and righteous in all your ways. We praise you for who you are.

Forgive us when we sin and fall short of your glory. We confess that we tend to want our own way.

Thank you for opening our hearts to receive you, God, as we humbly ask for you to fill us with your unselfish love. Thank you, Jesus, for what you did on the cross on our behalf. Will you guide, teach, and lead us on your path of righteousness as we trust you with our hearts? Fill us with the presence of your Holy Spirit in order to share this good news with others. Where the spirit of the Lord is, there is freedom.

# Let's Talk
## Conversations with Our Maker

*Devote yourselves to prayer, being watchful and thankful.*

—Col. 4:2

How can we develop a strong passion and a deepening pleasure of an intimate relationship with God through prayer? Knowing God and making him known is our highest calling in life. Prayer is conversing with God and getting to know him through his written word by his Spirit.

Jesus asks, "Who do you say I am?" (Mark 8:29). Do you know him?

How can we have an earnest desire to pray at all times? Desire can grow and develop into a flourishing prayer life within our own hearts as we intercede for others as well as ourselves (1 Thess. 5:16–19).

Let us encourage one another to incline our hearts to know God with the help of the Holy Spirit and to seek God with every fiber of our being. We can take shelter in him at church, in our homes, driving in our cars, in the workplace, in our neighborhoods, and within our families. May we come to cherish our Time Alone with God (TAG). Let's pray and practice thinking about what is pure and lovely and of good report (Phil. 4:8).

As we mature in our relationship with God through prayer, fasting, and meditation, we begin to recognize that we have stepped into a deeper, more powerful, supernatural realm. This new dimension of closeness with God will increase your faith and cause you to be more devoted to him. Your heart will be filled with his love, peace, comfort, and care for others as you develop the reflexes of Jesus.

As we abide with our Creator in prayer and meditation, we are drawn into an ever-present, conscientious awareness that God truly loves us. It's not saying that he loves us just to be saying it, but it's actually knowing it in our heart to be true and then daily living out that truth as we serve.

God is constantly near to us and has given us his guaranteed deposit of his presence through the Holy Spirit, pursuing us in an unbreakable, supernatural covenant (Ps. 25:14).

It is superbly powerful when an ever-increasing portion of a church body is brought to an understanding that God actually wants to hear their voices rising up to him in prayer.

So, let's pray!

*Because he has turned his ear to me, I will call on him as long as I live.*

—Ps. 116:2

If we believe that prayer is a powerful gift that is leading us into a sweeter affection for God and increasing our ability to hear his still, quiet voice, then why do we often hesitate to enter in? Why wouldn't we want to engage in continuous conversation with Jesus?

We know the answer to that question. It is our sins that keep us away from conversing with Jesus. Our flesh constantly rears its ugly head, and the battle is real. Sin is always crouching at the door, waiting to pounce on us (Gen. 4:7). Sin is familiar to us; it's what we do naturally, and we must fight every day against missing the mark.

By nature, we are fundamentally selfish and prideful. It is much easier to listen to the thousands of other voices clambering for our attention. We set up idols in our hearts over desiring the one true God. Consumerism and comparison are temptations for all of us since we tend to live our lives the way we want to. We live for our glory and don't act as if we understand that we are part of God's story instead of the other way around. We want total control, the control the world foists upon us every moment. The real truth is that we are a depraved, flesh-focused people in desperate need of a Savior.

We get so distracted by a world with thousands of advertisements extolling worldly things and worldly pleasures that we can quickly be distracted and soon forget that God is the Way, the Truth, and the Life.

> *He brought me out into a spacious place; he rescued me because he delighted in me.*
>
> —Ps. 18:19

> *All the ends of the earth*
> *will remember and turn to the LORD,*
> *and all the families of the nations*
> *will bow down before him,*
> *for dominion belongs to the LORD*
> *and he rules over the nations.*
>
> —Ps. 22:27–28

These scriptures are a reminder that he rescued us and that we will bow before him.

Years ago, I was on a worship team at a Methodist church in Tulsa, Oklahoma. We called ourselves the Pips (yeah, we had way too much fun) and met weekly for practice at the end of a workday. As we were going over our set one evening, I kept looking at the huge glass doors at the front of the sanctuary that were at my eye level. I could see the traffic flying by, car after car after car. It distracted me, and my mind began to wander.

Above the double doors that showed the outside world was an amazing, larger-than-life, 20-foot-high stained-glass window of Jesus. If you ever sat in the balcony, he was right there with you, looking over your shoulder.

Christ was standing with his outstretched arms and hands beckoning and receiving all people unto himself. It is still etched in my mind how beautiful the stained-glass window of Christ was that evening. The golden glow of the setting sun was streaming right through his hands and fingers. When I looked up at Jesus in his white robe, I saw a gentle, caring, loving smile, and I was engulfed by his love. I only saw Jesus beckoning to me, and soon, nothing else mattered. Peace flooded my soul.

You see, earlier that day, I had attended a funeral of a dear friend in that very room. God met me in the chapel that evening as the sun was setting. Jesus's hands and fingers were illuminated by a steady radiance of light streaming through the stained-glass window (Hab. 3:4). The warm glow from his hands, his wide-open hands, brought healing to my heartache (Ps. 34:18). My eyes and heart were set on him.

As we journey through this life, we get so preoccupied with *life*. It is a daily struggle to die to self and take up Christ's cross to follow his ways (Luke 9:23).

When we come to him with a heart of humility, he receives us just as we are, sin and all. You and I can come boldly into the abundant healing throne room of grace and converse with God. What I mean by this is that you can literally go to the throne room in your heart. Pray, and ask God to take you there after confessing your sins and asking God to draw you into his presence, focused on Jesus. Begin to envision in your mind's eye what heaven looks like from the perspective of the throne room of God. Read Revelation 21 and 22 to help you envision the beauty of heaven. It's right for us to be with him in quiet solitude.

Jesus is sitting right next to his Father, prevailing in prayer. Like a woman laboring during birth, Jesus is expectant for us to be in communication with him. Satan might be sifting you like wheat, but Jesus is ever interceding on your behalf (Luke 22:31–32). Scripture assures you that you matter to Jesus because he is praying for you. I don't always *see* things in heaven in my natural eye, but I experience the Lord's peace, grace, and mercy there. I see and experience Jesus in my heart. He is ever present with us.

The following men and women were great examples of entering into the presence of the Lord: Elijah (2 Kings 2:16), Enoch (Gen. 5:21–24), John (Rev. 20, 21, 22).

We read about Daniel's dreams and Ezekiel's visions and being lifted up in his spirit. We also read about Jeremiah's visions, Jacob's dreams, and his seeing God face-to-face (Gen. 31:11, 32:30). Many others in the Bible were lifted up in spirit and visited heaven. So why can't we enjoy his pleasures forevermore? Let us see Jesus in our hearts, minds, and spirits. He is bidding us to follow him, to know him, and to make him known.

We live in an upside-down kingdom, longing for eternity. When we spend time with him, we are causing our hearts and minds to be more like him. We can "turn our eyes upon Jesus, look full in His wonderful face, and the things of earth will grow strangely dim in the light of his glory and grace."[1] He is Lord. He has risen from the dead, and he is Lord.

When you spend time with someone, you get to know them. The more time you hang out together, the more you develop a relationship due to a deeper understanding of who they really are. It's a soul tie—a permanent connection. It can take years of developing an intimate friendship with someone for you to be raw and transparent about your life. There are also people who come into your life, and in an instant, you have a kindred spirit with them. You trust them and can therefore let your hair down and be real, completely honest about what's in your heart. You are even willing to risk sharing your struggles and confessing your sins with them in order to be healed (James 5:16). You will develop a bond that goes beyond the word *friendship*. It's the Spirit of the living God who connects you both in the unity of his Holy Spirit.

As you are spending time with God, getting to know him as you pray his names, attributes, and character, you will become acquainted with who he really is, and you will be changed in the light of his glory and grace. Out of an overflow of your heart, you will, in turn, want to make him known to those around you. Prayer should be a daily routine of an honest dialogue with God. Most importantly, it's listening to what he has to say to us.

---

1. Helen H. Lemmel, "Turn Your Eyes upon Jesus," Singspiration Music/ASCAP, 1922, https://library.timelesstruths.org/music/Turn_Your_Eyes_upon_Jesus/.

## See You at the Top

Hiking is an avenue, an adventure in which I immerse myself in nature. The higher the ascent up the mountain, the more I am profoundly engulfed by the presence of the Lord.

We need one another in the challenge of life here on earth. As we become a united body of believers in Christ with God-given gifts, we then can join together to honor and glorify our King.

Mt. Lononot is an amazing stratovolcano in the beautiful Rift Valley of Kenya. The trail on this mountain is straight up with no switchbacks or shade from the hot African sun. My guide, Jen, was right by my side during most of our quest to make it to the top. She also led the way for me to tread in her steps. Following my guide up the mountain soon left me covered by the dust of my sisters who were in the lead. That caused me to ponder what it might look like to be covered by Christ's attributes as I follow him. How sweet would it be to look like Christ in order for others to come to know him?

An amazing bond was formed as Jen and I sang songs, quoted scripture, and encouraged each other on this spectacular expedition. True community cares for and encourages one another no matter where you live or what language you speak.

Mt. Lononot, Rift Valley, Kenya, Africa

Around the age of 10, I began learning about the world map and missionaries who served God all over that map. When summer arrived, my family always visited the family farm in Oklahoma. I often would go outside to sit on the fence and watch the cows. Exciting, right? I loved the land and the fact that God entrusted us with that property.

A powerful thought crossed my mind. I asked God, "Please send me to Africa to be a missionary." I really wanted to go and serve God and the people I was learning about from my church.

In 2012, that simple statement I made as a child before the Lord eventually came to fruition.

Fifty some years later, I was honored to have that desire to go to Africa become a reality. Rachael Rosser asked my husband, Mark, and me to go to Africa in order to train key leaders with insight on biblical counseling in Lusaka, Zambia. Yes!

After a year of training, I received my biblical counseling certification and was ready to go and share this powerful knowledge. Our team took off for Africa only to learn more from our brothers and sisters in Zambia than we ever taught. When you study the Bible together, you bond together in a very deep and meaningful way. Our team taught the Zambians how to study the Bible inductively, which created a bond that cannot be broken.

Rachael has also led several teams to Kenya to teach and train trauma care to the women in the Rift Valley. I have been honored to be part of that team for several years now. We have come to know and love the women in Nakuru, Kenya, and our relationships have bonded into sisterhood. The courage and fortitude of these women in the midst of their great suffering and adversity are extraordinary. Their poverty that led to prostitution that led to Christ is truly a beautiful story of restoration in Christ. These sisters are strong, loving, kind, and faithful to the new work of the Lord in their lives.

Prayer changes things, so we pray, and in the process, we change. There are times when I am praying for the women of Kenya and Zambia and feel their prayers from around the world.

Our mornings should begin with "Dear God," and we should close out the day with "in Jesus's name, amen." Everything in between can be a continual prayer and listening to instructions from the Holy Spirit.

Jesus is the silent listener to our every conversation, so keep guard of your mouth and the source, the condition of your heart. In this concert of prayer throughout the day, you will feel a sweeter closeness to God as you commune with him in spirit.

We often sang this little song while we were on a Jamaica mission trip in 1974:

> Closer than a brother
> my Jesus is to me
> He's my dearest friend,
> He's everything I need.
> He's my rock, my shield and hiding place.
> Closer than a brother
> Jesus is to me![2] (inspired by Prov. 18:24)

From our first breath of life to the last time we exhale when our bodies give way and our spirits go to be with Jesus, let our hearts drink deep the breath of life *in* Christ.

Every day, we must preach and pray the gospel of peace to ourselves and to our brothers so we will remember what Christ accomplished on the cross. His death and resurrection are what our faith hinges on. That real doorway to salvation ushers in a relationship and freedom in the Spirit through Jesus Christ.

"The Way" (Acts 9:2, 24:14) is the answer to all of life. And when we preach the truth of the cross to ourselves daily, we soon find that out of the overflow of our heart, we share the gospel with passion to everyone we come in contact with. If not with words, then in sincere actions, we can give life to this generation of people filled with hurt, pain, and suffering. We can give them hope through the truth of who Jesus is and that he loves them and died for them to enable us to eventually spend all of eternity with him.

---

2. "Closer Than a Brother," *Gospel Choruses & Songs*, https://gospelchoruses.wordpress.com/2014/12/06/closer-than-a-brother/.

When we begin to comprehend that Christ went outside the perfect looking Jewish community to be crucified, we will see that he walked alongside the unlovable of society.

The lepers, the prostitutes, the foreigners, those who had broken the law—they were forced to reside outside the city gates. Those whose sins had caused them to live as refugees were outcasts and not part of any inner circle of the camp.

There was an awful stench in the air as the carcasses of the animals used for temple sacrifices were put in huge heaps outside the city limits. The blood of the animals flowed from the area where the remains burned daily, and as the smoke rose up to the heavens, it reeked of death. The conglomeration of sinful people living outside Jerusalem's walls was mainly the outcasts of society, and they stank to those of the inner circle of the law.

These outsiders became the eyewitnesses to the greatest act of love and obedience ever known to all humanity. It was with joy that Christ went to the cross in full submission to his Father, and the outsiders were right there to see and experience this miracle.

This is who we are—Gentiles, sinners, and outcasts. Once we were far off; now we are brought near to Christ (Eph. 2:13). Our fleshly manner and gross sins stink just like death and decaying flesh before we come to Christ, but now we have the fragrance of Christ on us. You and I once lived outside the holiness of God in the stench of our sins. Through Christ, we now show the mark of his high calling upon us.

We are all the same at the foot of the cross. His blood has redeemed us and made us new. God beckons us to be holy as he is holy. Now we reside in his camp—Camp Forgiveness. Let us be a sweet aroma to God where we live and move and have our very existence. The cross is Christianity; therefore, we are called to forgive, even for the deepest wounding.

What would it look like if we were a community distinguishable by a compassionate, persistent prayer life that truly changed us to be more like Jesus? I will even go further. What if we experienced a myriad of salvations, healthy marriages, heart's desires, and physical and spiritual healing in Jesus's name and for his glory?

As we experience the wonder of our Creator in a childlike manner, we commune with him with a purified heart and mind. Our childlike faith pleases him. "Let the little children come to me, and do not hinder them, for the kingdom of heaven belongs to such as these" (Matt. 19:14).

The apostles asked Jesus to teach them how to pray. We need to be schooled on how to pray as well. It is essential for us to devote ourselves to prayer in order to be forgiven as well as to forgive others (Matt. 6:9–13). Christ died on the cross for the sins of all people; God forgave us for our wicked hearts. Jesus is our example of how to be set free when we forgive those who trespass against us. But more importantly, prayer is the avenue to cherishing our Creator. When we fall in love with Jesus, we desire to follow his perfect ways and spend more time with him.

In John, chapter one, we learn that Philip is called to be a disciple, and then he quickly shares with his friend Nathanael, who is questioning whether anything good comes out of Nazareth. Philip beckons Nathaniel to also come and see Jesus. Nathaniel, after meeting Jesus, declares that Jesus is the Son of God. Once we meet and come to know Jesus, our lives are forever changed (John 1:43–51).

As believers of the Way, we too have access to go and experience the heavens open up and the angels ascend and descend on earth (Gen. 28:10–19). Prayer is the avenue to unlock our ability to see these greater things. Like Ezekiel, we can be lifted up in the Spirit and brought to the gate of the house of the Lord. Experiencing God is caught as we learn his exciting truths in his Word (Ezek. 11:1).

While the Apostle John was on the island of Patmos, God gave him an angel who testified to everything John saw. That is the Word of God and the testimony of Jesus Christ. John writes letters to the seven churches located in the Roman providence of Asia Minor to encourage them and instruct them in the way of the Lord.

> *After this I looked, and there before me was a door standing open in heaven. And the voice I had first heard speaking to me like a trumpet said, "Come up here, and I will show you what must take place after this." At once I was in the Spirit, and there before me was a throne in heaven with someone sitting on it.*
>
> —Rev. 4:1–2

14

John was able to glimpse into the throne room of heaven as he was literally able to come and see the mighty hand of the Lord at work concerning what is yet to come. The entire book of Revelation is summed up in its key verse, Revelation 1:1. The book of Revelation can be described as a nonlinear revelation of Jesus Christ by Jesus Christ. We are to know him, obey him, and walk in his love in order for the world to see Jesus.

With the gifts God has given his people, such as visions, dreams, discernment, and prophecy, we too have the possibility to visit God in the manner John did. We can begin to see things in the heavenly realm to encourage us to tell others of God's marvelous deeds. We may not actually see God face-to-face, but our spirit will bear witness to who he is and has been for all time. When you spend time with God in solitude, your heart begins to hear his voice in a clearer tone. The closer you get to his heartbeat, the more he entrusts you with hearing his voice.

Our granddaughter Remington is beginning to talk. It's babbling with a few words here and there, but regardless, she is sharing her thoughts with us. I have videos and live pictures of her looking up as her entire body is moving, along with her eyes, to see something flying in the air in our home. She oohs and aahs at what I believe are angels that are here to render service and minister to us (Heb. 1). I, too, have seen these messengers or hosts, or maybe even my guardian angel. I also believe that my mom saw angels around her in her last days here on earth.

Remington will not engage in a full conversation with us until she is older. However, we hope she will recall these encounters with heavenly beings when she is older. What is your first memory of the spirit world?

Since the Lord has set eternity in the hearts of all people, maybe, just maybe by seeing angels, we do experience him when we are too young to tell anyone. Does this sound possible for us today as followers of the Way? Why not? It is the same God who longs for us to long for him. He has truths that are revealed for those who seek him with all their hearts. They will find him. He is the same today, yesterday, and forever (Heb. 13:8). "Once more consider, there is nothing, but heaven, worth setting our hearts upon."[3]

---

3. M. Richard Baxter, *The Saint's Everlasting Rest* (Northampton, MA: Simeon Butler, 1819), 258, Google Books.

Fall on your knees.
Pour out your heart.
Lift up your hands before the Lord.
Pray.
Listen (Lam. 2:19, Ps. 62:8).

# Names, Character, and Attributes of God

**Names of God**

*Jehovah*

> The Self-Existent One
> I Am
> The true, eternal God
> The one who is
> Used 6,519 times in the Old Testament
> Translated Lord or Lord God

> Exodus 3:13–15
> Psalm 102:27
> Jeremiah 16:19–21
> 1 Chronicles 16:23–29
> Psalm 105:1–7
> John 8:58

*Jehovah Tsidkenu*

The Lord Our Righteousness

"There is no one righteous, not even one" (Rom. 3:10), but we have one who speaks to the Father in our defense—Christ Jesus, the righteous one. He is the atoning sacrifice for our sins.

1 John 2:1–2
Jeremiah 23:5–6
Romans 3:21–22
2 Corinthians 5:21
Ezekiel 36:25–26
Romans 5:17–19
1 John 1:7, 9

*Jehovah M'Kaddesh*

The Lord Who Sanctifies

*Sanctified* means set apart for holy use. It is the Holy Spirit who empowers us to live holy lives.

Exodus 31:12–13
Ephesians 4:11–16
1 Thessalonians 5:23–24
Leviticus 20:8
Philippians 1:6
1 Peter 2:9

*Jehovah Shalom*

The Lord Our Peace

"Therefore, since we have been justified through faith, we have peace with God through our Lord Jesus Christ" (Rom. 5:1).

Romans 5:1
Judges 6:22–24
Isaiah 26:3–4
Ephesians 2:14–18
Isaiah 9:6
John 14:27
Colossians 1:19–20

*Jehovah Shammah*
The Lord Is There
This name promises God's presence. "For where two or three gather in my name, there am I with them" (Matt. 18:20).
Deuteronomy 31:6
Ezekiel 48:35
1 Corinthians 3:16
Isaiah 12:6
Matthew 28:20
Revelation 21:1–3

*Jehovah Rapha*
The Lord Heals
God heals our bodies, but more importantly, he heals and restores our spirit and soul.

*Elohim*
The Triune God, Creator
Genesis 1:1
Psalm 95:1–7 Psalm 146:5–6
Isaiah 54:5
Isaiah 40:25–29
Colossians 1:15–19

*El Elyon*
The God Most High
Genesis 14:17–20
Psalm 47
Psalm 97:9
Psalm 7:17
Psalm 92:1–5
Psalm 148

*El Shaddai*

The Almighty, All-Sufficient God
>Genesis 17:1
>1 Chronicles 29:11–13
>2 Corinthians 12:9
>Hebrews 1:2–3
>Ephesians 1:19–21 Revelation 1:8

*El Olam*

The Everlasting God
>Genesis 21:23
>Psalm 102:11–12
>Hebrews 13:8
>Psalm 90:2
>Psalm 136
>Revelation 1:17–18

*Adonai*

The Lord and Master
>Deuteronomy 10:17
>Isaiah 45:22
>1 Corinthians 6:19–20
>Psalm 16:2
>Romans 14:7–9
>Revelation 5:9–10

*Father*

Distinguishing title in the New Testament
>Matthew 6:9–10
>John 14:6–11
>2 Corinthians 6:19–20
>John 10:27–30
>Romans 8:15–16
>1 John 3:1–3
>Exodus 15:22–26
>Psalm 103:1–4

Isaiah 53:4–5
Deuteronomy 32:39
Psalm 147:3
Matthew 8:16–17

## Jehovah Jireh

The Lord Will Provide

From the root word *to see*. God foresaw our need of redemption. This name tells us that God is willing and able to meet every need of his people.

Genesis 22:8, 13–14
Romans 8:32
Philippians 4:19
Acts 14:17
2 Corinthians 9: 8
1 Timothy 6:17

## Jehovah Rohi

The Lord Our Shepherd

*Rohi* is also translated "companion" or "friend."

Psalm 23
Ezekiel 34:14–16
John 10:11, 27–28
Isaiah 40:11
Matthew 18:12–13
Revelation 7:17

## Jehovah Nissi

The Lord Our Banner

*Nissi* is also translated "ensign" or "standard" and represents God's cause, his victory.

Exodus 17:15–16
Psalm 60:4
Isaiah 11:10
Psalm 20:5–8
Song of Solomon 2:4
1 Corinthians 15:56–57

*Jehovah Sabaoth*
The Lord of Hosts
Commander of all the armies of heaven

Deuteronomy 20:1–4
Nehemiah 9:5–6
Zechariah 14:9
1 Samuel 17:42–47
Psalm 103:19–22
Revelation 11:15

*El*
The God of Power and Might

Exodus 15:1–3, 11
2 Chronicles 20:6
Psalm 89:5–8
Deuteronomy 3:24
Psalm 18:2–3
Isaiah 43:10–13

## God's Character

*Love*

Psalm 136:1–9
Romans 5:5–8, 8:35–39
1 John 3:1, 4:7–10
Ephesians 3:16–19

*Light*

Psalm 104:1–2, 119:105
John 8:12
2 Corinthians 4:6
1 John 1:5–7
Revelation 21:22–25

*Our Father*

Deuteronomy 1:30–31
Psalm 68:4–5
Luke 11:11–13
John 1:12–13
2 Corinthians 6:18
Galatians 4:4–7

*Our Joy*

1 Chronicles 16:27–33
Nehemiah 8:9–12
Psalm 4:7–8; 30:1–5, 11–12; 43:3–5
Zephaniah 3:17

*Miracle Worker*

1 Chronicles 16:8–12
Psalm 77:11–14, 111:2–5
Luke 7:20–23
John 20:30–31, 21:25

*Compassionate*

Nehemiah 9:16–21
Matthew 7:24–25
1 Corinthians 10:4
2 Samuel 22:47
Psalm 18:31–36, 46–50; 62:1–8
Psalm 103:8–14, 145:8–9
Isaiah 30:18, 49:13–16
Matthew 9:36
1 Samuel 2:1–2

*Shield*

2 Samuel 22:1–4, 36
Psalm 3:1–3
Psalm 5:11–12
Psalm 115:9–11
Psalm 84:10–12
Proverbs 2:7–8

*Fortress*

Psalm 18:1–3
Psalm 91:1–8
Proverbs 14:26
Psalm 59:16–17
Psalm 144:1–2
Jeremiah 16:19

*Friend*

Exodus 33:11
Isaiah 41:8–10
John 15:9–17
Proverbs 18:24
Mark 3:31–35
James 2:23

*Counselor*

Psalm 119:24
Isaiah 28:29
John15:26
Isaiah 9:6
John 14:16–17, 25–27
John 16:7–15

*Comforter*

Psalm 23:4
Psalm 94:17–19
Matthew 5:4
Psalm 71:17–22
Isaiah 66:13
2 Corinthians 1:3–5

*Communicator*

1 Samuel 3:9–10
Isaiah 30:19–21
John 10:27–28
Job 33:13–18
Matthew 10:18–20
1 Corinthians 2:9–13

*Savior*

Psalm 68:19–20
Matthew 1:21
Titus 3:3–6
Isaiah 43:11–13
Acts 5:30–31
1 John 4:14–15

*Deliverer*

2 Samuel 22:17–20
Psalm 34:1–7, 15–19
Isaiah 46:3–4
Psalm 22:4–5
Psalm 91:9–16
2 Corinthians 1:8–10

*Merciful*
> Micah 7:18–20
> Luke 6:35–36
> Ephesians 2:3–9
> Luke 1:46–55
> Romans 9:14–16
> Titus 3:5–7

*Intercessor*
> Job 16:19–21
> 1 Timothy 2:5
> Hebrews 9:24
> Romans 8:26–27, 33–35
> Hebrews 7:25
> 1 John 2:1
> Deuteronomy 32:1–4
> Psalm 12:6
> Isaiah 25:1
> 2 Samuel 22:31
> Psalm 19:7
> Matthew 5:48

*Way*
> 2 Samuel 22:31–34
> Isaiah 48:16–17
> John 14:4–7
> Psalm 16:11
> Isaiah 55:6–9

*Truth*
> Psalm 119:160
> John 8:32
> John 17:3, 17
> John 1:17
> John 16:13
> 1 John 5:20

*Life*
> Deuteronomy 30:19–20
> John 5:21
> John 11:25–26
> Nehemiah 9:6
> John 6:35, 47–51
> Acts 17:25

*Victor*
> Deuteronomy 20:1–4
> Psalm 44:1–8
> Proverbs 21:30–31
> Joshua 21:43–45
> Psalm 118:13–17
> 1 Corinthians 15:51–57

*Hope*
> Isaiah 40:28–31
> Lamentations 3:21–25
> Hebrews 6:17–20
> Jeremiah 29:11–13
> Romans 15:4–13
> 1 Peter 1:3

## Attributes of God

### God Is Eternal

Without beginning or end; existing through all time; everlasting

Exodus 3:14–15

John 8:58

Nehemiah 9:5 Psalm 93:2

Romans 1:20

Exodus 15:18

Psalm 45:6

Isaiah 26:4

1 Timothy 1:17

Deuteronomy 33:27

Psalm 90:1–3

Jeremiah 31:3

Revelation 1:8, 18

### God Is the Creator

The one who brought the universe and all matter and life into existence

Genesis 1:1

Psalm 104

Jeremiah 10:12

Colossians 1:16

Psalm 95:3–7

Psalm 148:1–6

John 1:3

Hebrews 1:3

Psalm 100:3

Isaiah 42:5

Acts 17:24–28

Revelation 10:6

### God Is Good

Virtuous, excellent, upright; God is essentially, absolutely, and consummately good

Psalm 25:8

Psalm 34:8

Psalm 85:5

Psalm 119:68

Psalm 136:1

Psalm 145:9

Jeremiah 33:11

Nahum 1:7

Mark 10:18

John 10:11

1 Timothy 4:4

2 Peter 1:3–4

### God Is Omniscient

Having infinite knowledge; knowing all things

Psalm 44:21

Psalm 147:5

Matthew 6:8

Romans 11:33–34

Psalm 139:1–6

Isaiah 65:24

Matthew 10:30

Colossians 2:3

Psalm 142:3

Daniel 2:22

John 6:64

Hebrews 4:13

*God Is Omnipresent*
Present at all places at all times
    1 Kings 8:27
    Psalm 139:5–12
    Matthew 28:20
    Colossians 1:17
    Psalm 31:20
    Isaiah 66:1
    Acts 17:27–28
    2 Timothy 4:16–18
    Psalm 46:1–7
    Jeremiah 23:24
    Romans 8:35, 38–39
    Hebrews 13:5

*God Is Immutable*
Never changing or varying;
unchangeable
    Numbers 23:19
    Psalm 100:5
    Isaiah 40:6–8
    Hebrews 6:17–19
    1 Samuel 15:29
    Psalm 102:25–27
    Isaiah 52:6
    Hebrews 13:8
    Psalm 33:11
    Psalm 119:89, 152
    Malachi 3:6
    James 1:17

*God Is Good*
God is supreme, highest in rank,
power, authority; superior, highest
in degree; utmost
    Genesis 14:19
    Job 11:7–9
    Isaiah 44:6–8
    Hebrews 1:4, 6
    Deuteronomy 10:14–17
    Psalm 95:3–7
    Acts 17:24–28
    Jude 24–25
    Nehemiah 9:6
    Psalm 135:5
    Colossians 1:15–18
    Revelation 4:8

*God Is Sovereign*
Holding the position of ruler, royal,
reigning; independent of all others;
above or superior to all others; con-
trols everything, can do anything
    1 Samuel 2:6–8
    Job 42:2
    Psalm 93
    Isaiah 46:9–10
    1 Chronicles 29:10–13
    Psalm 33:10–11
    Psalm 135:6–7
    Matthew 10:29–30
    2 Chronicles 20:6
    Psalm 47:2–3, 7–8
    Isaiah 40:10
    Romans 8:28–29

## God Is Omnipotent

All powerful, having unlimited power or authority, almighty

> 2 Chronicles 32:7–8
> Psalm 147:5
> Habakkuk 3:4
> Ephesians 3:20
> Psalm 62:11
> Isaiah 40:28–31
> Matthew 19:26
> Colossians 1:10–12
> Psalm 89:8–13
> Jeremiah 32:17
> Ephesians 1:19–20
> Hebrews 1:3

## God Is Faithful

Constant, loyal, reliable, steadfast, unwavering, devoted, true, dependable

> Deuteronomy 7:9
> Psalm 119:90
> Lamentations 3:21–24
> 2 Timothy 2:13
> Psalm 33:4
> Psalm 145:13
> 1 Corinthians 10:13
> 1 John 1:9
> Psalm 89:8
> Psalm 146:5–8
> 2 Timothy 1:12
> Revelation 19:11

## God Is Holy

Spiritually perfect or pure; sinless; deserving awe, reverence, adoration

> Exodus 15:11
> 1 Samuel 2:2
> Psalm 77:13
> Psalm 99
> Psalm 111:9
> Isaiah 5:16
> Isaiah 57:15–16
> Luke 1:49
> Acts 3:13–15
> 1 Peter 1:15–16
> Revelation 4:8
> Revelation 15:4

## God Is Just

Right, fair, impartial, upright, lawful, correct, true, righteous

> Deuteronomy 32:4
> 2 Chronicles 19:7
> Psalm 9:7–10
> Psalm 89:14–16
> Psalm 119:137–138
> Psalm 145:17
> Isaiah 30:18
> Zephaniah 3:5
> John 5:30
> Romans 3:25–26
> 2 Thessalonians 1:5–7
> Revelation 15:3–4

*God Is Wise*

From the root *to know* or *to see*, but wisdom goes past knowledge to understanding and action; having keen perception, discernment; power of judging rightly; always making right choices

1 Chronicles 28:9

Proverbs 2:6

Isaiah 55:8–9

Romans 16:27

Psalm 92:5

Proverbs 3:19–20

Daniel 2:20–22

Colossians 2:2–3

Psalm 147:5

Isaiah 28:29

# A.C.T.S.

*Praise be to the name of God for ever and ever; wisdom and power are his. He changes times and seasons; he deposes kings and raises up others. He gives wisdom to the wise and knowledge to the discerning. He reveals deep and hidden things; he knows what lies in darkness, and light dwells with him. I thank and praise you, God of my ancestors: You have given me wisdom and power, you have made known to me what we asked of you, you have made known to us the dream of the king.*

—Dan. 2:20–23

**Adoration** – of a holy God, his name above all others
**Confession** – of the Holy Spirit to cleanse us from sin
**Thanksgiving** – for a kingdom to come and for our daily provision
**Supplication** – forgiveness of sins both of commission and omission, both spoken and unspoken. Rescue us, Lord, from tribulation in the name of Jesus.

## Jesus Prays
Pray in Jesus's name and with his resurrection power.
  Jesus prayed before meals – Luke 24:30

Jesus prayed for others – John 17:9
Jesus prayed with others – Matthew 18:20
Jesus prayed for us – John 17:20
Jesus prayed alone – Luke 5:16

## A.C.T.S.

Below are four steps on how to pray the names, attributes, and character of God.

Coming to know God is when you pray who he is.

A = Adoration – Matthew 6:9, Psalm 145:3, Psalm 66:1–2

C = Confession – 1 John 1:9

T = Thanksgiving – Colossians 3:17

S = Supplication and Intercession – John 15:7

**A** – Using God's names, his attributes, and his character to worship and adore him through prayer is the pattern of the four steps of prayer known as A.C.T.S.

He is God, and we must acknowledge his supremacy.

In that mindset, spend 20 minutes praising God for who he is.

There is a distinctive difference between adoration and thanksgiving. This time is set up to honor God. Thanking him for what he is doing comes after confession.

This pattern is seen throughout the Bible, acknowledging God for who he is, admission of our sins, and thanking him for all he is doing. Then we intercede for others. Daniel 9, Luke 11:1–4

**C** – After reading, praying, and focusing on praising God, we come to grips with the fact that we certainly fall short of God's glory. For the next five minutes or so, set aside your pride and silently confess your sins before God. If you feel led to openly confess your shortcomings before others, I suggest that you do so with a home group or with a person of high integrity. First John 1:9 is a beautiful mystery of his love and forgiveness for us.

**T** – Thanksgiving is a sweet time of gratefulness unto the Lord. For the next 15 minutes, thank God for what he is doing in your life, your family, and the life of the church. Watch out not to make this a time of broad strokes interceding for others. This is a time set aside to concentrate and hone in on a central theme.

**S** – For the last 20 minutes of the hour of power, make supplications on behalf of others. Lift up your family, friends, pastors, community, and government, and stand in the gap for the lost. Pray for the nations. Pray for others—it is such a privilege. When you say amen, you will be a changed person. Your heart and body will feel the peace of God that surpasses all understanding.[1] This form of praying is found throughout God's Word.

---

1. A.C.T.S. is adapted from *Moms in Touch International Leadership Manual*, 1994, www.momsinprayer.org.

# The Old and the New

*But I, by your great love, can come into your house;*
*in reverence I bow down toward your holy temple.*

—Ps. 5:7

*And foreigners who bind themselves to the LORD to minister*
*to him, to love the name of the LORD, and to be his servants,*
*all who keep the Sabbath without desecrating it and who hold*
*fast to my covenant—these I will bring to my holy mountain*
*and give them joy in my house of prayer. Their burnt offerings*
*and sacrifices will be accepted on my altar; for my house will be*
*called a house of prayer for all nations.*

—Isa. 56:6–7

Joy in the house of prayer. I want that kind of jubilation in my heart and in yours for the life of believers in Christ. Delight can come about when we bind ourselves to the Lord, as we love his name and worship him. We once were far off as foreigners and have been gathered in as we hold fast to God and worship him. We will receive joy as we draw near to him.

## Hannah

Let's take a look at Hannah and her heart-wrenching earnest plea before the Lord. This prayer is a beautiful model of lamenting before God.

*Then Hannah prayed and said:*

> *"My heart rejoices in the LORD;*
> > *in the LORD my horn is lifted high.*
> *My mouth boasts over my enemies,*
> > *for I delight in your deliverance.*
>
> *"There is no one holy like the LORD;*
> > *there is no one besides you;*
> > *there is no Rock like our God.*
>
> *"Do not keep talking so proudly*
> > *or let your mouth speak such arrogance,*
> *for the LORD is a God who knows,*
> > *and by him deeds are weighed.*
>
> *"The bows of the warriors are broken,*
> > *but those who stumbled are armed with strength.*
> *Those who were full hire themselves out for food,*
> > *but those who were hungry are hungry no more.*
> *She who was barren has borne seven children,*
> > *but she who has had many sons pines away.*
>
> *"The LORD brings death and makes alive;*
> > *he brings down to the grave and raises up.*

*The L*ORD *sends poverty and wealth;*
    *he humbles and he exalts.*
*He raises the poor from the dust*
    *and lifts the needy from the ash heap;*
*he seats them with princes*
    *and has them inherit a throne of honor.*

*"For the foundations of the earth are the L*ORD*'s;*
    *on them he has set the world.*
*He will guard the feet of his faithful servants,*
    *but the wicked will be silenced in the place of darkness.*

*"It is not by strength that one prevails;*
    *those who oppose the L*ORD *will be broken.*
*The Most High will thunder from heaven;*
    *the L*ORD *will judge the ends of the earth.*

*"He will give strength to his king*
    *and exalt the horn of his anointed."*

—1 Sam. 2:1–10

Big Bend National Park, Chisom Mountain, Texas

## Reflection

*But the Advocate, the Holy Spirit, whom the Father will send in my name, will teach you all things and will remind you of everything I have said to you.*

—John 14:26

1. Ask the Holy Spirit to teach you as you read the passage.
2. Read and reread this passage. Ask God to reveal truth to your heart in what he longs to speak to you through his Word.
3. Do you sense a deeper closeness to God?

## TAG

*The LORD confides in those who fear him;*
*he makes his covenant known to them.*

—Ps. 25:14

Choose a name of God, one of his attributes, or a character of God. Look up the related scriptures, read them, and pray them. Ask God to speak directly to you.

*Open my eyes that I may see*
*wonderful things in your law.*

—Ps. 119:18

Date _____ Attribute _____

Definition _____

Scripture _____

_____

What does this mean to you personally? _____

Ask God, "How does this apply to me, Lord?" _____

Write a prayer thanking God for the specific thoughts he has impressed upon you today.

## Write out your prayer requests for today:

_____

_____

_____

_____

_____

_____

_____

_____

_____

_____

_____

_____

_____

_____

_____

Hannah is a tremendous example of a woman who sought after Yahweh, the covenant-keeping God, during her deepest time of pain and suffering. Hannah's story is one of hope through heartache. In her bitterness of soul, Hannah prayed for a son and vowed to give him to the Lord to serve in his temple.

Hannah's husband, Elkanah, had two wives, Hannah and Phinehas. We read that Hannah was barren while Phinehas had several children. The scriptures also reveal that Phinehas provoked and irritated Hannah daily, probably because Elkanah loved Hannah and gave her a double portion of the meat during sacrifice and worship to the Lord. Every day, Hannah interacted with Phinehas who bullied her for not having any children and for being favored by their husband. Hannah must have been greatly oppressed, yet in her suffering, she turned to God for comfort. Her weapon of defense was to pray. This is where we need to be encouraged and follow her example of praying through difficult situations and not let our hurt and pain allow us to sit in a sinful pity party.

Hannah had a relationship with Yahweh and sought after him as she wept and fasted. Even though she was barren, Hannah remained faithful to God and his covenant with her. When it seemed as if God was silent, Hannah was faithful to pour out her heart before the Lord in prayer. Elkanah, in the midst of his wife's anguish, supported her with comfort and assurance and showed her that he loved her no matter what the circumstances.

Hannah also had to deal with bitterness in her heart, that root of shame and anger that can run deep from the trauma of being wounded. Hannah pressed into the Lord through prayer in the dark night of her soul. She was comforted by the Holy Spirit, waited for an answer, and stood firm until she received the favor of the Lord upon her life. God blessed Hannah with a son—Samuel—and out of gratitude, she dedicated her son to the Lord.

All along, God had a plan for Hannah's life in her obedience toward him. God allowed this story of suffering to unfold before so many people in the book of 1 Samuel that in the end, everyone was very aware that only God could do this mighty deed. God always has a plan for our good and for his glory. We don't always see it, but that is where faith comes into play. Faith will build us up in our innermost being. Faith is believing more than we know.

Samuel became one of the greatest prophets in the Old Testament. He prayed, listened to God, and obeyed the voice of God.

There were five women in the Old Testament who were barren, and God showed his loving grace as he opened up their wombs for the births of Isaac, Jacob, Joseph, Samson, and Samuel. That is why we read our Bibles. Indeed, there are many encouraging stories of faith through trials and suffering.

It is inspirational to know that we stand right alongside these patriarchs through our momentary afflictions. Prayer, fasting, worship, and weeping cause us to move our hearts closer to God's heart. God knows suffering. His Son excruciatingly suffered for all humankind.

## Daniel

*We do not make requests of you because we are righteous, but because of your great mercy.*

—Dan. 9:18

Let's take a look at the book of Daniel, chapter nine, for an example of what prayer can look like no matter what situation you are in. From exile to freedom, God is with us.

The back story is that the Israelites walked in disobedience before God and his commandments. God allowed them to live in exile in Babylon under King Nebuchadnezzar due to their sins against the Lord. Daniel was one of the young men taken into captivity and was known for his reputation of high integrity. He had great wisdom and was well educated. He and his friends were placed in the king's court, and they earned favor with the king. There is so much in the book of Daniel that I want to encourage you to read and study. It's an amazing narrative of Daniel's life, God's people, and the end times.

In Daniel 9, we come to understand what stirred Daniel's heart to pray to God. He was interceding on behalf of the Israelites and himself since they were displaced from their homeland. God's people had been rebellious and sinned against God, which is why he allowed their captivity.

We also walk in disobedience to the Lord, and He will allow us to do so. He will give us over to our sinful nature in order for us to turn back to him later in great need. He always takes us back into the fold with open arms and everlasting love. He is a covenant-keeping God. The question is this: Will we keep our covenant with him?

Daniel had been reading Jeremiah, one of the prophets in the Torah. He came to understand that the Lord had told Jeremiah that the desolation of Jerusalem would last 70 years.

From this, Daniel realized that the 70 years of the Israelites' captivity were almost completed. So Daniel got on his knees and prayed, probably facing a window toward the east as was his practice three times a day (Dan. 6:10). Daniel had a relationship with God and thus knew this covenant-keeping King personally. He knew exactly how to pray.

Daniel's Prayer:

> *In the first year of Darius son of Xerxes (a Mede by descent), who was made ruler over the Babylonian kingdom—in the first year of his reign, I, Daniel, understood from the Scriptures, according to the word of the LORD given to Jeremiah the prophet, that the desolation of Jerusalem would last seventy years. So I turned to the Lord God and pleaded with him in prayer and petition, in fasting, and in sackcloth and ashes.*

> *I prayed to the LORD my God and confessed:*

> *"LORD, the great and awesome God, who keeps his covenant of love with those who love him and keep his commandments, we have sinned and done wrong. We have been wicked and have rebelled; we have turned away from your commands and laws. We have not listened to your servants the prophets, who spoke in your name to our kings, our princes and our ancestors, and to all the people of the land.*

> *"Lord, you are righteous, but this day we are covered with shame—the people of Judah and the inhabitants of Jerusalem and all Israel, both near and far, in all the countries where you have scattered us because of our unfaithfulness to you. We and our kings, our princes and our ancestors are covered with shame, LORD, because we have sinned against you. The Lord our God is merciful and forgiving, even though we have rebelled against him; we have not obeyed the LORD our God or kept the laws he gave us through his servants the prophets. All Israel has transgressed your law and turned away, refusing to obey you.*

*"Therefore, the curses and sworn judgments written in the Law of Moses, the servant of God, have been poured out on us, because we have sinned against you. You have fulfilled the words spoken against us and against our rulers by bringing on us great disaster. Under the whole heaven nothing has ever been done like what has been done to Jerusalem. Just as it is written in the Law of Moses, all this disaster has come on us, yet we have not sought the favor of the LORD our God by turning from our sins and giving attention to your truth. The LORD did not hesitate to bring the disaster on us, for the LORD our God is righteous in everything he does; yet we have not obeyed him.*

*"Now, Lord our God, who brought your people out of Egypt with a mighty hand and who made for yourself a name that endures to this day, we have sinned, we have done wrong. Lord, in keeping with all your righteous acts, turn away your anger and your wrath from Jerusalem, your city, your holy hill. Our sins and the iniquities of our ancestors have made Jerusalem and your people an object of scorn to all those around us.*

*"Now, our God, hear the prayers and petitions of your servant. For your sake, Lord, look with favor on your desolate sanctuary. Give ear, our God, and hear; open your eyes and see the desolation of the city that bears your Name. We do not make requests of you because we are righteous, but because of your great mercy. Lord, listen! Lord, forgive! Lord, hear and act! For your sake, my God, do not delay, because your city and your people bear your Name."*

—Dan. 9:1–19

"Please take note that Satan is not afraid of our preaching the word of Christ, yet how very much he is in fear of our being subject to the authority of Christ."[1]

---

1. Watchman Nee, *Spiritual Authority* (New York: Christian Fellowship Publishers, 1972), 9, Google Books.

## Reflection

*But the Advocate, the Holy Spirit, whom the Father will send in my name, will teach you all things and will remind you of everything I have said to you.*

—John 14:26

1. Ask the Holy Spirit to teach you as you read the passage.
2. The pattern in the prayer is A.C.T.S.
   - A – adoration
   - C – confession
   - T – thanksgiving
   - S – supplication

3. Read Jeremiah 29:10–11. What is the Holy Spirit revealing to you in that passage?
4. Ask who, what, when, where, and how questions.
5. What have you taken away from spending time in Daniel, chapter nine? Do you sense a deeper closeness to God? Has your own prayer life been enhanced? Do you grasp how high and wide and deep his love is for you? Take time to read and also pray Daniel 9:4–19. Yes, I know it is one of the longest prayers in the Old Testament. Remember, it is based on God's promises, and Daniel unlocks truth because he knew God and his Word.

## TAG

*The LORD confides in those who fear him;*
*he makes his covenant known to them.*

—Ps. 25:14

Choose a name of God, one of his attributes, or a character of God. Look up the related scriptures, read them, and pray them. Ask God to directly speak to you.

*Open my eyes that I may see wonderful things in your law.*
—Ps. 119:18

Date _____ Attribute _____

Definition _____

Scripture _____

_____

What does this mean to you personally? _____

Ask God, "How does this apply to me, Lord?" _____

Write a prayer thanking God for the specific thoughts he has impressed upon you today.

**Write out your prayer requests for today:**

---

---

---

---

---

---

---

---

---

---

---

---

---

---

In Daniel 9:17–19, we read Daniel's words of authenticity before the true King. Here, we learn of Daniel's compelling statement of honesty and humility in his request to God. This can be our declaration, too—humility poured out before the Lord in spirit and in truth. His mercy endures forever (Ps. 136).

> We do not make requests of you because we are righteous, but because of your great mercy. Lord, listen! Lord, forgive! Lord, hear and act! For your sake, my God, do not delay, because your city and your people bear your Name.
>
> —Dan. 9:18–19

Here is what we can learn about Daniel in God's beautiful words. Daniel runs to God to guide him in all truth. That same gift is there for us to grasp today. We have a holy God who wants to hear from us, and he does speak to us by his Word as well as by the presence of the Holy Spirit.

Daniel confides in God. He is communicating with his maker, asking for guidance and confirmation of what he just read in the book of Jeremiah. He is pleading for a release from the 70-year exile in a foreign land, for God's people wanted to go back to Israel.

Daniel knows where his loyal citizenship is. It's not only in Israel, but ultimately it is in heaven. We, too, have the very same home that Daniel longed for, but in the meantime, we are here in boot camp on earth. We are earthly beings who are ultimately heaven-bound but on earth for now. Our true home for all eternity will be a renewed earth.

While Daniel is praying, he has a vision. The angel Gabriel comes to Daniel and gives him instructions and understanding. Don't you want that kind of prayer life? I do! With hands raised high as we talk to God in a personal way, we are to listen intently to hear his voice clearly. You and I can walk in the truth that is produced by an ongoing desire to know him. God uses his Word to speak to us. Remember, the Word of God is alive and active; it penetrates our heart and changes us to be more like Christ.

The first thing the angel does is affirm what kind of man Daniel is, saying he is highly esteemed by God. What kind of person we are matters. Our character matters to God, our family, and even ourselves. We, too, need to be people of integrity. We are to embody a trustworthiness that honors God and reflects him to a lost and dying world full of people living in exile.

Then Gabriel tells Daniel to consider, to observe, and to pay attention to the message and understand the vision. Later, in Daniel, chapter 10, we read about another angel, Michael, who comes to help Daniel in his time of need, giving him strength and peace. Michael had been warring in the heavens for 21 days against the prince of the Persian kingdom as Daniel was prevailing in prayer. There was a battle going on, and prayer was an appeal for victory.

I have had several visitations with angels over the years that have left no doubt in my mind and heart that God had a message for me through these encounters. God speaks to us in mysterious, supernatural ways. Throughout the Bible, we read about angels and the heavenly hosts. We don't hold them in a higher regard than Christ, but they are created to come alongside us, render service, and minister to us. Hebrews, chapter one, tells us that angels are messengers from the Lord. The hosts of angels you read about in the Bible are God's warring army. They are assigned to render services and minister to us. When you pray, you can ask for their help and assistance (Ps. 148:2, Heb. 1:7, 14).

God desires to be ever present and near to us. So we need to enter into his presence on purpose. We can come and see Jesus. We can draw near to him, and he will draw near to us (James 4:8). What we learn in the original Hebrew language is that the definition of the word *see* means seeing the warrior prince in the Spirit now.

Daniel was in a relationship with God. He spent time with God in word, prayer, meditation, and praise. Daniel repented of his sins and made intercession on behalf of the nation of Israel for their sins. He sought God in all things, from his eating habits to how he conducted business. Most importantly, Daniel listened to the voice of the Lord. He was obedient to the call. When you have intimacy with God, you will hear from him. A sensitive and obedient heart hears the voice of the Lord.

The bottom line is that Daniel loved God and walked in obedience to him. The top line of the gospel is that God loved Daniel, and He loves us, too. He is intimately acquainted with us and knows who we are (Ps. 139).

Do you desire to love God with all your heart, soul, and strength? If so, you will be compelled to regularly spend time with him in prayer and meditation.

Here's the really hard part: Listen to God, and obey his commandments. I want to encourage you that this is a lifetime of walking with God in his fullness that will cause you to bear meaningful fruit. From your first step in faith to fully relying on God in all things, you can have a closer walk with God. Come to know this Christ, for he is the Creator of all things; you are made in his image, and he desires to talk with you.

We can make our petitions known to God at any time for all people. When we are praying for the nations, the lost, and our enemies, we will line up with the heartbeat of God. We can enter into his presence to hear his whispers of love and care for his creation.

## David

> *People look at the outward appearance, but the LORD looks at the heart.*
>
> —1 Sam. 16:7

David is another patriarch in the Old Testament who captures my attention. David is tagged as a man after God's own heart. David knows God intimately and makes him known to the nations. David is the youngest son of Jesse and will be appointed by God to be the king of Israel. Even when David grossly sins, he repents and cries out to God to not take the presence of the Holy Spirit from him.

> *Search me, God, and know my heart;*
> *    test me and know my anxious thoughts.*
> *See if there is any offensive way in me,*
> *    and lead me in the way everlasting.*
>
> —Ps. 139:23–24

> *Do not cast me from your presence*
> *    or take your Holy Spirit from me.*
>
> —Ps. 51:11

David was not a perfect man, yet he was a man who when convicted of his sins, repented and turned from his sinful nature and then became even more dedicated to worship the Lord with all his heart, soul, and strength (Deut. 6:4–7).

A ruddy and handsome young shepherd who lived under the open skies with the intensity of the elements, David poured out his heart before God, writing songs, poetry, and yes, even his concerns and complaints. What you behold, you become. David beheld the beauty of nature, and not only did he see God, but he experienced him. Out of those encounters with God, David began to write poetry and sing of God's majesty.

In the book of 1 Samuel, we quickly learn how brave David was time and time again. In chapter 17, we read that David ran into the battlegrounds where fighting was taking place against the Philistines. Remember that David did not say, "I will kill this Goliath." Instead, he made a strong statement to the Israelites about Goliath and God (1 Sam. 17:26).

*Who is this uncircumcised Philistine that he should defy the armies of the living God?*

—1 Sam. 17:26

David believed that the battle was God's to win. He knew and served a living God. The Word of God is living, active, and alive (Heb. 4:12).

David could make this statement because he knew God would win the battle. God is alive, and David knew it. The Hebrew language is a living dialect, and it brings life to us today. When the nation of Israel was looking for a king and their hearts were far from God, they elected a king. During that time, David was spending time with God in an open field, taking care of sheep.

David's youth was spent in the rock-filled fields near his hometown, Bethlehem. He was abiding in those fields with the family's sheep, tending to their needs. He protected the sheep and cared for them daily. David led his sheep in the right, safe path they traveled. He kept predators at bay from the family business of sheepherding. He carried a club and a staff to use for protection over the flock. When the wolves came after the little ewes, David would chase them away and, if necessary, kill the alpha of the pack.

Rift Valley, Kenya, Africa

When David came to an open field with green grass for the lambs to eat, he would go before the sheep and remove stones and obstacles so the sheep would not get hurt as they grazed and thrived in the fields. He would even go so far as to fill holes with dirt so the lambs would not fall and injure themselves as they went into the field to eat. David prepared a table for his flock.

David anointed their heads with oil, keeping the flies out of their eyes and keeping them free from disease. They needed to keep their eyes fixed on David, their shepherd, as he poured the oil on them. David carried both a rod and a staff. The staff indicated he was the lead shepherd over the flock; he kept the rod ready to correct the sheep when they steered away from their master.

He led the sheep alongside still waters to drink. If they had not yet been sheared, their coats would be thick and oversized. If the sheep drank from the stream of rushing waters while heavily coated with their wool, they could easily fall into the river and drown as their coats became drenched, pulling them down into the rushing waters. I am sure David rescued many of his flock at the precise time from the rushing water that was pulling them away from their Shepherd.

Still waters were much easier for the lambs to drink from, providing a peaceful and safe time to drink the life-giving waters. David would lead them by the still waters to drink often. We, too, need to drink from the rivers of life in order to be washed and cleansed by the Word of God and be sanctified (Eph. 5:26).

There were even times when David would have to make the sheep rest, sleep, and not overeat. Sometimes they would want to keep grazing all day and all night. Overeating was not uncommon for most of the sheep. David had to make them lie down in green pastures, stop, and take a Sabbath. We too must lie down and recover from our work in order to serve God with all our strength.

David spent countless hours playing the harp and singing before God. The music must have calmed the little lambs to rest in peace and comfort. At dusk, David would gather the sheep into a rock wall pen or maybe one made of sticks as a place to corral them for the evening. David would lie at the one and only entrance of the pen to be the guardian of the door and keep the sheep safe. He became the door of safety.

If one of the 100 sheep wandered off as they did time and time again, David would leave the 99 of the flock to rescue one. I'm so thankful for that because I'm that one.

> Prone to wander, Lord, I feel it,
> Prone to leave the God I love;
> Here's my heart, O take and seal it,
> Seal it for thy courts above.[2]

Discipline comes with a cost. David would find the lost sheep that had more than likely wandered off more than once, and then he would break one of its legs to keep it from wandering off again. He would bind up the broken leg and then place the ewe around his neck. For the next several months, he would carry that lamb on his shoulders until the leg healed. Can you imagine the relationship they must have developed? David tenderly and lovingly cared for this sheep. All the sheep were totally dependent on

---

2. Robert Robinson, "Come Thou Fount of Every Blessing," *Indelible Grace Hymn Book*, http://hymnbook.igracemusic.com/hymns/come-thou-fount-of-every-blessing.

the shepherd. He disciplined and cared for each lamb with compassionate love. Are you crying yet? This is us. Jesus loves us so much that he is willing to allow us to wander away from him. He will discipline us, breaking our selfishness, in order to achieve obedience from us, those who are called true believers. If this will cause us to get back into fellowship with him, he will carry us from the breaking point all the way to healing and beyond.

What does this have to do with prayer? Everything! God is our Shepherd and longs for us to be in his flock, walking in obedience. He yearns for a relationship with us. He desires to take care of us. He protects, feeds, leads, and anoints us. He watches over us. He is our caring, loving Shepherd who leaves the 99 for the one. The good, good Shepherd hears our cries. He hears our prayers. He restores our souls. He loves us, and even when we go astray, Christ is near, lovingly waiting for us to come. He binds up our brokenness. He holds us close—if we allow him to.

When I was in Kenya recently, I stepped back 2,000 years. The sweetest memories were made while I was in the Rift Valley where the shepherd boys still guide their flocks of sheep to graze alongside the road. These young shepherds had a staff in one hand and a rod in the other hand to lead, guide, and discipline these not so smart animals. I marveled at the simplicity and beauty of the kinship between the sheep and their shepherd. It stirred my affections for the Lord, and I worshiped God with a deep and abiding joy.

Picture this in your heart. He is your Shepherd, you shall not want. God loves you, and this Shepherd—your Shepherd—takes care of you in all of life, no matter the cost. The cost was his Son's life for you and for me.

He is your defender, caretaker, provider, and protector. He is the night watcher and the one who will sing over you with songs of deliverance with a gentle love. With exceedingly great joy, this Shepherd guides you to the right places to feed you and cause you to trust, love, rest in him, and believe in him as your astonishing leader, your Shepherd (Zeph. 3:17).

David loved nature and writing music to the Creator of the universe. He took care of his flock and did what it took to keep them safe as he cared for them. He emulated Christ.

We, too, can be like Christ, caring for others and guiding them into God's perfect character. To know our Shepherd and make him known is indeed the calling for every believer in Jesus Christ.

*A psalm of David when he was in the desert of Judah*

> *You, God, are my God,*
>> *earnestly I seek you;*
> *I thirst for you,*
>> *my whole body longs for you,*
> *in a dry and parched land*
>> *where there is no water.*
>
> *I have seen you in the sanctuary*
>> *and beheld your power and your glory.*
> *Because your love is better than life,*
>> *my lips will glorify you.*
> *I will praise you as long as I live,*
>> *and in your name, I will lift up my hands.*
> *I will be fully satisfied as with the richest of foods;*
>> *with singing lips my mouth will praise you.*
>
> *On my bed I remember you;*
>> *I think of you through the watches of the night.*
> *Because you are my help,*
>> *I sing in the shadow of your wings.*
> *I cling to you;*
>> *your right hand upholds me.*
>
> *Those who want to kill me will be destroyed;*
>> *they will go down to the depths of the earth.*
> *They will be given over to the sword*
>> *and become food for jackals.*
>
> *But the king will rejoice in God;*
>> *all who swear by God will glory in him,*
>> *while the mouths of liars will be silenced.*

—Ps. 63:1–11

## Reflection

> *But the Advocate, the Holy Spirit, whom the Father will send in my name, will teach you all things and will remind you of everything I have said to you.*
>
> —John 14:26

1. Ask the Holy Spirit to teach you as you read the passage.
2. What is the Holy Spirit revealing to you in this passage?
3. Has your prayer life been enhanced by this scripture? Do you grasp how high and wide and deep his love is for you?

## TAG

> *The LORD confides in those who fear him;*
> *he makes his covenant known to them.*
>
> —Ps. 25:14

Choose a name of God, one of his attributes, or a character of God. Look up the related scriptures, read them, and pray them. Ask God to directly speak to you.

> *Open my eyes that I may see*
> *wonderful things in your law.*
>
> —Ps. 119:18

Date _____ Attribute _____

Definition _____

Scripture _____

_____

What does this mean to you personally? _____

Ask God, "How does this apply to me, Lord?"_____

Write a prayer thanking God for the specific thoughts he has impressed upon you today.

## Write out your prayer requests for today:

_____

_____

_____

_____

_____

_____

_____

_____

_____

_____

_____

_____

_____

David is calling on God, praising him for who he is—his Elohim, holy and true.

David's soul (Hebrew: *nepes*) was indicating breath and life that is thirsty for God. David is parched within his soul and longing for fulfillment in his spirit.

David's body and flesh are longing and yearning for God, the Creator of his very existence. There is a tether, a connection and a beautiful bond between David's heart and the heart of God.

You are no different since God has also placed eternity in your heart. Do you see it? Can you feel his presence? You are made in his image, the Imago Dei, so it makes sense that your relationship with God is embedded in your heart and soul, and truly, that is what your heart longs for.

David has seen (Hebrew: *hazah*) God in the sanctuary. Hold on here! Let's investigate and unpack this statement in order to look, see, and behold God as David did in Psalm 63. To gaze and to prophesy—this word *seen* is used to denote both a vision and a revelation given to God's prophets. The sanctuary here is not only a place but also something most consecrated unto God. David saw God and saw what God was doing in the sanctuary. We can go into the sanctuary through prayer every day if we desire to see our Shepherd.

To know God and be known by God (like David was striving for) is a magnificent example for us today as we press into the Lord. We, too, can have this intimate, holy, sanctuary-type relationship with God as we look to the examples of the patriarchs. God wants us to have an authentic understanding and reality where God calls us friend. This causes my heart to enlarge. We can have this blessed close bond; all we need to do is seek his face (his will) in prayer, worshiping and coming to know him as we read his Word. David saw his power and his glory.

We have also seen God's power and glory—at the cross and when Jesus was in earnest prayer in the garden seeking guidance from his Father.

God's love (Hebrew: *hesed*) is better than life. This love denotes kindness and mercy that comes from a close friend, a ruler, and our true King. The word *hesed* is central to God's character and closely tied to his covenant with his people. This is his loving covenant agreement with us, filled with his mercy and kindness.

When we look with a Hebrew perspective at the Old Testament, we see in the Psalms that David knows God as Creator. He knows the names of God and the character of God. David is satisfied in God alone. The riches of the world will not compare to the praises sung from David's lips to his God.

When David became king of Israel, his sole pursuit was to bring the presence of the Lord back to the city of David.

Not only did David go down to Obed-Edom's household to bring the Ark of the Covenant back to Jerusalem, but he also ushered in God's presence as he danced undignified before the city. Think about this: When they got the Ark of the Covenant in their possession and began the journey home, it was 50 kilometers (31 miles) from Obed-Edom's home.

Scripture informs us that the men carrying the Ark of the Covenant stopped after taking only six steps to sacrifice a bull and a fattened calf. Some scholars say it was every six steps, from start to finish, that a sacrifice was being made. No matter if it was only six steps and a one-and-done sacrifice or thousands of sacrifices made by the priests along the way, it indeed was a blood sacrifice unto the Lord. David's clothes would have been stained from the bloody offerings. So that explains his drunken behavior as he danced, twirled, and worshiped his King as he entered the city. As David was surrendering an animal to cover his sins and the sins of the people, his worship intensified. Hebrews 12:28–29 reminds us to worship God with thankfulness and awe, for he is a consuming fire.

David was filled with the presence of the Lord. He was elated that the precious Ark was honored by coming to rest in the city of David to bless the kingdom (2 Sam. 6). What would it look like if we could grasp the bloody sacrifice of Christ on the cross and then be filled with his presence in order to dance before our King? Note that David was solely focused on honoring the presence of God and his glory. He was not trying to use the Ark as a lucky charm the way the Jewish people and Saul had tried to use it (1 Samuel and 2 Samuel).

All David wanted to do was to delight with singing underneath the shadow of God's wings. This shadow is God's shelter, and it offers protection from our enemies. The bottom line is that David was praying to know God in a deeper and more intimate way. He was growing in his relationship with his Maker. The top line is that God loved David's songs of praise to him.

The joy of discovering God's Word for your heart as you read, study, meditate, chew on, and rest in Psalm 63 is that you will find comfort.

Do you want your life to be full and satisfying regardless of your ongoing circumstances? Oh, how God longs for your friendship, voice, and praise! Ask the Holy Spirit to guide you in all truth and love as you become more intimately acquainted with your Creator, the very Maker of heaven and earth. Only God can truly satisfy our longings and desires. He is all we need. We need nothing else. If all we have is God, that is enough.

Jesus is the good Shepherd, and his love for you is unmatched by any other love.

> He tends his flock like a shepherd:
>   He gathers the lambs in his arms
> and carries them close to his heart;
>   he gently leads those that have young.
>
> —Isa. 40:11

The Lord is my shepherd, I lack nothing.

—Ps. 23:1

## Jesus

> I am the good shepherd; I know my sheep and my sheep know me.
> —John 10:14

> During the days of Jesus' life on earth, he offered up prayers and petitions with fervent cries and tears to the one who could save him from death, and he was heard because of his reverent submission.
> —Heb. 5:7

There is no greater example in the Bible than Christ and his conversations with his Father. It begins in the book of Genesis and is still going on at this very moment for your life and mine.

Jesus is seated at the right hand of God the Father, ever interceding for us (Rom. 8:34). Jesus is prevailing in prayer like a woman laboring in childbirth. Take comfort in knowing that Jesus cares for you and is praying on your behalf right now. Satan might be sifting you like wheat, but Jesus is ever interceding on your behalf.

When God stated in Genesis 1:26, "Let us make mankind in our image, in our likeness," the Hebrew word *ruah* (spoken) meant Spirit and breath, wind and air. It was the Spirit of the Lord hovering over the waters. And then God spoke creation into existence.

Jesus and the Holy Spirit were there when God's breathing brought about the creation of the universes. Prayer is conversation and devotion, so creation is an invocation, the act of invoking something or someone for assistance or as an authority. It was a supernatural event.

Creation is likened unto prayer. Maybe that is why I adore creation and prayer so much.

Throughout God's Word, we see the three-in-one. The dance of the Trinity is always working together—separate only in function. God has always existed. He is infinite. Therefore, the Father, the Son, and the Holy Spirit are blended as one, each distinct in his own magnificence (Gen. 1:26).

Throughout the Old Testament, we learn that there are 400 prophecies, appearances, and foreshadowings of Jesus. He is revealed throughout the entire Old Testament. We have the privilege on this side of the cross to know that most of those prophecies have already come to fruition. It is with great expectation that we await his return and the completion of the work of the cross—the consummation of all things. It's Friday, but Sunday's coming!

Jesus was always looking to the Father to see what he was doing. When Jesus was 12 years old, attending Passover with his parents, he stayed behind without Joseph and Mary realizing it. After asking friends and family where Jesus could be, his parents returned to Jerusalem only to find him dialoging with the teachers in the temple. Mary said, "Son, why have you treated us like this? Your father and I have been anxiously searching for you." Jesus responded, "Why were you searching for me? . . . Didn't you know I had to be in my Father's house?" (Luke 2:48–49). Jesus was compelled and drawn to be in his Father's house. He was about his Father's work. Jesus's baptism was quite the event; as he came up out of the water, the heavens opened up, and the Spirit of God descended upon him like a dove. "A voice from heaven said, 'This is my Son, whom I love; with him I am well pleased'" (Matt. 3:17).

Some ancient scholars indicate that when the early church baptized new followers of the Way, converts would walk down several steps into the water if a river was not nearby. The water would be flowing and not stagnant. The decision you made to trust in God is a gift, and by the power of the Holy Spirit, it is God who redeems you, not the water. The symbol of the water is an act of obedience, an outward sign of an inward change of heart. You walk into the living waters alone, engulfed by the power of the Spirit to come up out of that water walking in new life.

Following Christ's baptism, the Holy Spirit led him into the desert for 40 days and nights to be tempted by Satan. Daily we are tempted by the enemy's schemes. How we combat the deceiver is up to us. Is it our way or God's way? The Word of God will not return void. Every time Satan tried to lure Jesus into sinning, Jesus answered with scripture, saying, "It is written" (Matt. 4:4).

Scripture brings strength and truth to help us in the fight against the enemy. Jesus himself used God's Word to fight this battle (Matt. 4:1–11). There is a point in these narratives that shows us that throughout Christ's life, prayer is what he embraced. He spoke to his Father continually.

If we read scripture with a prayerful heart and with our minds in tune with God's Word, we will have a deepened relationship with Christ. We follow Christ's example of how he conversed with his Father. When we join in the fellowship of his suffering, his death, and his resurrection, we truly grasp the power of his name and the finished work of the cross. Be compelled to know Christ and the power of his proven resurrection from the grave.

Jesus prayed often. Jesus prayed in nature. He was passionate. His prayers were heartfelt. Jesus's prayers were the Word of God. His prayers were persistent. Jesus prayed alone. He asked his garden friends (eye-witness disciples) to pray for him. Jesus prayed for God's will to be done. Jesus is praying right now for you and me.

Let's read more about Christ's life, obedience, and prayerful conversations with his Father. All these facts about Jesus's life are in all the Gospels.

His ministry in Galilee – Matthew 4:12–18:35

His transfiguration – Matthew 17:1–8

On his way to Jerusalem – Mark 19–20

In Jerusalem – Luke 19:28–21:38

The Last Supper – John 13–17

His arrest and trial – Matthew 26:36–27:31

The Crucifixion – Luke 23:26–55

Jesus's resurrection and appearances – John 20–21

These passages include his miracles and major teachings, and his disciples and apostles did benefit from his prayer life. His spoken word and acts of healing were done in his name in humble submission and in conversational prayer to his Father. Get to know your Jesus.

As you read and study the Bible, your eyes will be opened to the greatest story ever told, the true story of God. The Holy Spirit will lead and guide you into all truth when you ask for his Spirit to lead you.

### Jesus Prayed for Himself

The book of John awakens our minds to a greater understanding that Jesus is truly the Son of God, the light of the world. After 400 years of darkness and people not hearing the voice of God through angels, priests, or prophets, John the Baptist comes on the scene and says that "in him was life, and that life was the light of all mankind. The light shines in the darkness, and the darkness has not overcome it" (John 1:4–5). Jesus is the light of the world that takes away the darkness of sin. Light entered the scene after 400 years of darkness and silence.

In John 15, we read that Jesus is the true vine and his Father is the gardener. I would love to expand on chapter 15, but for now let's look at the chapters we will be looking at as snapshots leading us right up to Jesus and how he prays. Let's look at a very important find in verses 16 and 17 of chapter 15 in the Gospel of John. He chooses us and appoints us to bear fruit that will last.

To be God's delegated authority is not merely to manifest a little of resurrection, but it is to have the rod sprout, bloom, and bear fruit, this becoming matured resurrection life.[3]

Jesus then gives a command to his disciples to love each other. Today, Jesus is asking us the same thing: Are we his disciples? If so, let's remember the call to love one another today.

Jesus reminds the disciples that the world will hate them and persecute them for his name's sake. Jesus begins to talk to them about the Counselor, the Spirit of truth, coming to give them power.

Take time as you read God's Word to look very closely at the word *Spirit*. What is God telling you here? Pay close attention. Ask the Holy Spirit to direct you to the truth in this power-packed Word. This is a great time to do a word study of *Spirit*. Look up all the scriptures in a book of the Bible for *Holy Spirit*, and journal what you learn.

In John 16, we read about the work of the Holy Spirit as Jesus is talking to his band of brothers. In verse 13, we see that when the Spirit of truth comes, he will guide you into all truth—not some truth but *all* truth. Come, Holy Spirit, come.

The disciples couldn't comprehend the words Jesus spoke to them since he was explaining his impending departure from them and that he was going to be with his Father. He begins to explain to the disciples that because they loved him and believed in him, God loved them, too. A light bulb went off in their heads and hearts, and they got it. They once were blind, and now they could see. Jesus asked the disciples, "Do you now believe?" (John 16:31).

*After Jesus said this, he looked toward heaven and prayed: "Father, the hour has come. Glorify your Son, that your Son may glorify you. For you granted him authority over all people that he might give eternal life to all those you have given him. Now this is eternal life: that they know you, the only true God, and*

---

3. Watchman Nee, *Spiritual Authority* (New York: Christian Fellowship Publishers, 1972), 146, Google Books.

*Jesus Christ, whom you have sent. I have brought you glory on earth by finishing the work you gave me to do. And now, Father, glorify me in your presence with the glory I had with you before the world began."*

—John 17:1–5

*Jesus Prays for His Disciples*

*"I have revealed you to those whom you gave me out of the world. They were yours; you gave them to me and they have obeyed your word. Now they know that everything you have given me comes from you. For I gave them the words you gave me and they accepted them. They knew with certainty that I came from you, and they believed that you sent me. I pray for them. I am not praying for the world, but for those you have given me, for they are yours. All I have is yours, and all you have is mine. And glory has come to me through them. I will remain in the world no longer, but they are still in the world, and I am coming to you. Holy Father, protect them by the power of your name, the name you gave me, so that they may be one as we are one. While I was with them, I protected them and kept them safe by that name you gave me. None has been lost except the one doomed to destruction so that Scripture would be fulfilled.*

*"I am coming to you now, but I say these things while I am still in the world, so that they may have the full measure of my joy within them. I have given them your word and the world has hated them, for they are not of the world any more than I am of the world. My prayer is not that you take them out of the world but that you protect them from the evil one. They are not of the world, even as I am not of it. Sanctify them by the truth; your word is truth. As you sent me into the world, I have sent them into the world. For them I sanctify myself, that they too may be truly sanctified."*

—John 17:6–19

*Jesus Prays for You*

*"My prayer is not for them alone. I pray also for those who will believe in me through their message, that all of them may be one, Father, just as you are in me and I am in you. May they also be in us so that the world may believe that you have sent me. I have given them the glory that you gave me, that they may be one as we are one—I in them and you in me—so that they may be brought to complete unity. Then the world will know that you sent me and have loved them even as you have loved me.*

*"Father, I want those you have given me to be with me where I am, and to see my glory, the glory you have given me because you loved me before the creation of the world.*

*"Righteous Father, though the world does not know you, I know you, and they know that you have sent me. I have made you known to them, and will continue to make you known in order that the love you have for me may be in them and that I myself may be in them."*

—John 17:20–26

## *Reflection*

> *But the Advocate, the Holy Spirit, whom the Father will send in my name, will teach you all things and will remind you of everything I have said to you.*
>
> —John 14:26

1. Ask the Holy Spirit to teach you as you read the passage.
2. Now look for keywords and phrases. Highlight them in different colors. Father—joined together—love.
3. Is there a pattern in these prayers?

## TAG

> *The LORD confides in those who fear him;*
> *he makes his covenant known to them.*
>
> —Ps. 25:14

Choose a name of God, one of his attributes, or a character of God. Look up the related scriptures, read them, and pray them. Ask God to directly speak to you.

> *Open my eyes that I may see*
> *wonderful things in your law.*
>
> —Ps. 119:18

*Teachings on Prayer by Jesus*

> *Jesus answered, "I am the way and the truth and the life. No one comes to the Father except through me."*
>
> —John 14:6

Date _____ Attribute _____

Definition _____

Scripture _____

_____

What does this mean to you personally? _____

Ask God, "How does this apply to me, Lord?"_____

Write a prayer thanking God for the specific thoughts he has impressed upon you today.

## Write out your prayer requests for today:

_____

_____

_____

_____

_____

_____

_____

_____

_____

_____

_____

_____

_____

_____

One of the disciples walked over to Jesus as he finished praying and asked, "Would you teach us a model prayer that we can pray, just like John did for his disciples?" So Jesus taught them this prayer:

*One day Jesus was praying in a certain place. When he finished, one of his disciples said to him, "Lord, teach us to pray, just as John taught his disciples."*

*He said to them, "When you pray, say:*

*"'Father, hallowed be your name, your kingdom come.*
*Give us each day our daily bread.*
*Forgive us our sins,*
*    for we also forgive everyone who sins against us.*
*And lead us not into temptation.'"*

—Luke 11:1–4

God is the center of our lives as the Holy Spirit fills us and purifies us. We should desire his kingdom here on earth while God takes care of us each and every day.

When we come to grips with our own sins and know in our hearts that we are pardoned from our transgressions, we can sincerely forgive others. Due to our forgiving Father's love, we in turn will desire to emulate Christ and forgive others.

Christ took on all sins—past, present, and future sins of all people. He went to the cross in obedience, joy, and love to forgive us of all the wrongs we commit daily. The cross must be the place we see and grapple with when we think of the fact that we too need to die to self due to our pride and forgive our brothers and sisters.

Forgive ourselves, forgive those who have wronged us, forgive those whose sins upon us have left us scarred. There is therefore no greater lesson than the truth of the cross and how it personifies forgiveness.

As believers, we can walk in freedom when we leave our sin, our hurts, and our pain at the foot of the cross, never to be picked up again. Peace that surpasses all understanding is forever ours as we guard our hearts and minds in Christ Jesus.

# Listen Up

## Hearing the Voice of the Lord

> *For the word of God is living and active. Sharper than any*
> *double-edged sword, it penetrates even to dividing soul and*
> *spirit, joints and marrow; it judges the thoughts and attitudes*
> *of the heart.*
>
> —Heb. 4:12

God speaks to us through his written Word. The Bible is sufficient to give us what we need to live godly lives. Here are several ways we can hear God's message to us personally. Several of these examples and scriptures came from attending the 2001 Convergence Conference in Oklahoma City, Oklahoma.[1]

## 1. God's Word

> *"Your word is a lamp for my feet, a light on my path."*
> —Ps. 119:105

---

1. Sam Storms, *Equip Convergence Guidebook* (Oklahoma City, OK: Bridgeway Church, 2001), www.bridgewaychurch.com.

God speaks directly through his Word to you. His Word is his authority. His Word is sharper than any two-edged sword; it can fillet us open and fill us with truth. God uses the Holy Spirit to speak to us in our spirit as we read and discern his precepts. God's Word will not return void (Isa. 55:11). God's Word is the way, the truth, and the life (John 14:6).

## 2. Clear Voice of the Lord

> *As soon as Jesus was baptized, he went up out of the water. At that moment heaven was opened, and he saw the Spirit of God descending like a dove and alighting on him. And a voice from heaven said, "This is my Son, whom I love; with him I am well pleased."*
>
> —Matt. 3:16–17

God speaks with Abraham – Genesis 22:1–2, 10–12
God spoke to Moses – Exodus 3:3–6
The nation of Israel – Deuteronomy 5:22–24
Samuel – 1 Samuel 3:1–10
Elijah – 1 Kings 19:11–13
He spoke to John the Baptist – Matthew 3:16–17
Peter, James, and John – Matthew 17:5–6, 2 Peter 1:17–18
The general public – John 12:27–30
Paul – Acts 10:9–16
John – Revelation 1:9–12
God speaks to us in our hearts by the Holy Spirit – Judges 13

## 3. Inner Voice of the Lord

> *My sheep listen to my voice; I know them, and they follow me.*
> —John 10:27

It is that small, still voice that you hear in your heart and in your spirit; you know that you know it is God.

Romans 10:17, Jeremiah 33:3, John 8:47, Isaiah 30:21, John 16:13, John 6:63, Psalm 32:8–9, John 14:16–17, James 1:19–27, 2 Timothy 3:16–17, John 14:26, Romans 8:14

## 4. Angelic Message-Bearer

*Now an angel of the Lord said to Philip, "Go south to the road— the desert road—that goes down from Jerusalem to Gaza."*
—Acts 8:26

God declares His message to us through angelic messengers. These angels pronounced God's desires to:

Joshua – Joshua 5:13–15
Samson's parents – Judges 13
Isaiah – Isaiah 6:6–13
Daniel – Daniel 9:20–27
Zechariah – Luke 1
Mary – Luke 1
Philip – Acts 8:26
Peter – Acts 5:19–20
Others – Hebrews 3:1

The first words out of the angels' mouths in the Old Testament were, "Fear not." These amazing beings are the messengers that bring good news, fight our battles, and steer us onto the correct path.

## 5. Dreams

The Lord communicates to us in our dreams: Genesis 20:3, 37; Daniel 2, 4, 7; Matthew 1, 2; Acts 2, 10. Today, we are witnessing many Muslims and other people groups coming into the faith of God through dreams and visions by seeing a white-hot Jesus. When you have dreams that come from God, you will remember every detail of the images.

When you have dreams that come from the Lord, most often someone else is gifted in interpreting them. When I share with a few of my wisest friends the vivid details that are impressed on my mind from dreams, it's not long after I share with them that they can interpret the meaning.

## 6. Visions

*Listen to my words:*

> *"When there is a prophet among you,*
> *I, the LORD, reveal myself to them in visions,*
> *I speak to them in dreams."*

—Numbers 12:6

Daniel 10:1–9; Acts 2:17, 9:10–12, 10:1–6, 10:9–16, 16:9–10, 18:9–10, 22:17–18

A vision is a picture or series of events that come either while a person is sleeping or in meditation before the Lord. If you have visions or dreams from the Lord, write them down. When these revelations come to you, they are sealed in your mind and heart. That's one way you know that they are from God. They are for building up the body of Christ.

I want to share a few personal visions I have experienced over the years. These experiences encourage me in my daily walk with the Lord and remain in my heart to glorify him.

*April 19, 2020*
*A vision from God in the middle of the night*
Suddenly I was flying straight up into the dark sky of midnight.

I recall thinking this: Am I dreaming, or is this a vision? Is this really happening?

It didn't matter what to call this experience; it was real, and I became captivated by it.

Billions of brilliant stars were zooming past me against the blackened sky.

Some of the stars were small and luminous; others were bright white and of considerable size.

These burring balls of fire were in present time, not from a millennium ago. They flickered in the glow of pure white in the moment.

As I was accelerated upward, all I could do was smile. I was filled with joy and great peace.

I was by myself yet I did not feel alone.

This ultra-fast journey upward was a gift, a beautiful fulfillment of truth in my heart.

The third heaven opened, and time stood still.

I went from acceleration to floating in midair.

My body was different, as if I were only in the Spirit.

Immediately, I was engulfed by a myriad of huge angels so much so that they were all I could see.

The angels were massive.

Their wings were feathers—white with silver-grey brushing among their pinions (the outer part of a bird's wing, including the flight feathers).

Some of the angels were flying, while others covered me.

All I saw were wings both great and small.

I didn't hear anything, yet I knew the holy ones had engulfed me (Luke 9:26).

Earthly words cannot describe what I saw, experienced, and felt while I was in heaven.

I briefly saw my granddaughter's face pop up among the many white angel wings. She was with the host of guardian angels and was being protected by them.

I believe some of the angels I saw were the very ones I have called on to war and protect our home and our family on a daily basis (Heb. 1).

In an instant, an impression of the deceiver's face was there. I didn't actually see or focus on him. He reared his ugly head, yet I was not afraid.

The warring angels covered over me.

Immediately, my mind went to Ephesians 6:10–19 and Job 1:6–12.

I knew that the enemy roams in the heavenly places, but soon he will no longer be able to do so.

"The Spirit and the bride say, 'Come!" (Rev. 19:11–22:21).

Come, Lord Jesus. Come!

*March 7, 2020*
*The Tree of Trust*

As a child, I loved climbing trees and sitting on a high branch for a long time to daydream and pretend. Most days, you would find me singing gospel hymns out loud and talking privately with God. I believed that every time I scurried up that tree, I was closer to God. Maybe I didn't consciously know that's what I was doing. I just knew I desired time alone in the clouds with God.

⸱ This dream was incredible timely and, once again, a gift from the Lord.

I was in a beautiful, lush forest—tall, green grass aligned with hundreds of huge trees. The bark of the trees was light brown with dark knots within the growth. They looked like aspen trees only with the green leaves of an oak tree.

There was a large treehouse in the forest that housed our neighbors from Tulsa. The pastor's home was filled with children, laughter, and peace. There was a warm meal being prepared for later, so I stepped outside for a while. Immediately, I was back in the lush forest, and everything else faded away.

One large tree covered everything I saw. Its roots were spread throughout the landscape, so I began to climb. Childlike once again, there was a drive in me to go as high as I could climb the branches. As I was making my assent, suddenly there were no reachable tree limbs to grab hold of. In fact, all limbs were gone, even those to assist me back down. I became gripped with fear. How will I survive?

Immediately, that big tree began to hold me. It formed into a reclining place for me to rest within its large trunk. I relaxed, and fear was completely gone.

Assurance flooded my soul, and peace flooded my heart.

My Father and I were one. I understood in my heart, soul, and strength that he was covering me.

This scripture filled every fiber of my being:

> Trust in the LORD with all your heart
> and lean not on your own understanding;
> in all your ways submit to him,
> and he will make your paths straight.
>
> —Prov. 3:5–6

Psalm 37 and 91

*March 1, 2018*
*S.H.*
I saw a large, wooden map of the United States of America. This picture took up my entire mind's eye.

In the heart of the map was the state of Texas. There was a huge handprint in red, like finger painting. The hand imprinted on the map was Steve's hand. The red color represents the blood of the Lamb.

The imprint was an open hand, outstretched from the wrist to the tip of the fingers. The hand was on Dallas. This hand was pointing up on the map going north toward Canada.

There were much smaller handprints that were covering every state in the United States. All the hands went out from Texas. Some states had several handprints permeating them.

Even though the map took up all I could see, I also saw hands going off the map into the seas and beyond.

We are the hands and feet of Christ.

You are God's willing and obedient servants.

Steve, the way you love others is contagious. You pour out your love and his love unto others as Christ has gifted you with deep passion. Your life has impacted thousands, and your influence on them has impacted another thousand and beyond. Your dedication to God's Word and prayer is a living legacy.

A map is a symbolic depiction emphasizing relationships between elements of some space such as objects, regions, or themes.

I see this map as spiritual, indicating how you have touched the lives of men and women across this great nation and beyond. The ministry God has placed in your care has been one that exceeds time and space.

It's not just what you have spoken into these lives but how you have moved them to action. You have counseled with and prayed for thousands. You have inspired and spurred on all of us to love others and have passion for the city we live in.

You have spent countless hours directing and leading us to care for the lost.

You have made Christ's name famous, not only among the church but also to those in need of a forgiving Savior.

Your humble heart literally produces more than it can handle, yet you leave nothing behind. You give your all.

Matthew 28:16–20

## 7. Nature and Creation

*The heavens declare the glory of God;*
    *the skies proclaim the work of his hands.*
*Day after day they pour forth speech;*
    *night after night they reveal knowledge.*
*They have no speech, they use no words;*
    *no sound is heard from them.*
*Yet their voice goes out into all the earth,*
    *their words to the ends of the world.*
*In the heavens God has pitched a tent for the sun.*
    *It is like a bridegroom coming out of his chamber,*
    *like a champion rejoicing to run his course.*
*It rises at one end of the heavens*
    *and makes its circuit to the other;*
    *nothing is deprived of its warmth.*

*The law of the LORD is perfect,*
    *refreshing the soul.*
*The statutes of the LORD are trustworthy,*
    *making wise the simple.*
*The precepts of the LORD are right,*
    *giving joy to the heart.*
*The commands of the LORD are radiant,*
    *giving light to the eyes.*
*The fear of the LORD is pure,*
    *enduring forever.*
*The decrees of the LORD are firm,*
    *and all of them are righteous.*

*They are more precious than gold,*
*than much pure gold;*
*they are sweeter than honey,*
*than honey from the honeycomb.*
*By them is your servant warned;*
*in keeping them there is great reward.*
*But who can discern their own errors?*
*Forgive my hidden faults.*
*Keep your servant also from willful sins;*
*may they not rule over me.*
*Then I will be blameless,*
*innocent of great transgression.*

*May these words of my mouth and*
*this meditation of my heart*
*be pleasing in your sight,*
*LORD, my Rock and my Redeemer.*

—Ps. 19:1–14

God reveals himself through nature. From the stars to the mountains and the sea, he is displaying himself to be known, loved, and revered. We are made in his image. God is our Creator, and he longs for us to worship him with every fiber of our being.

## Reflection

> *But the Advocate, the Holy Spirit, whom the Father will send in my name, will teach you all things and will remind you of everything I have said to you.*
>
> —John 14:26

1. Ask the Holy Spirit to teach you as you read the passage.
2. Now look for keywords and phrases. Highlight them in different colors.
3. Share with others what you have learned about God.
4. Apply to your life what you have experienced and learned from God's Word.

## TAG

> *The LORD confides in those who fear him;*
> *he makes his covenant known to them.*
>
> —Ps. 25:14

Choose a name of God, one of his attributes, or a character of God. Look up the related scriptures, read them, and pray them. Ask God to directly speak to you.

> *Open my eyes that I may see*
> *wonderful things in your law.*
>
> —Ps. 119:18

Date _____ Attribute _____

Definition _____

Scripture _____

_____

What does this mean to you personally? _____

Ask God, "How does this apply to me, Lord?"_____

Write a prayer thanking God for the specific thoughts he has impressed upon you today.

## Write out your prayer requests for today:

_____

_____

_____

_____

_____

_____

_____

_____

_____

_____

_____

_____

_____

_____

_____

I love my Father's world. The mountains declare his glory as they shoot upward to the heavens with their snow-covered, jagged caps. The mountains declare his glory with their fields of colorful wildflowers and the crystal-clear blue lakes. The bears and rams roam on top of mountains over the boulders to claim the wilderness as their home.

Oceans are teeming with sea creatures, filling the vast expanse of the sea. The shores crash with sounds like a mighty roar as the waters move with force. The warm, white sands of the beach bring healing as you walk on the shore.

Oh, how the atmosphere sings of his praise while the white, fluffy clouds dance on the backdrop of a baby-blue, robin's-egg sky. The heavens declare his glory at all times, the beautiful sky above that can change and deepen in many shades of blue to show the vast array of God's breath. The very wind that you can't see is God's display of his living presence for us to experience by the movement of the trees it blows upon.

The stars' dazzling blaze of lights fills the night's darkness with brilliance and guidance. Those same stars led wise men to seek Jesus.

There is the mysterious moon and its pull on earth as it waxes and wanes, bursting with light as it's in full bloom, and the narrow strips that still light up the evening sky with a sliver of hope. The moon's color changes from white to yellow and blood red, signifying heavenly signs from the Lord.

As you walk through a forest, its trees blaze with the seasonal changing of color from green, yellow, red, and brown and the fullness of leaves to bare sticks called limbs. The whole earth declares God's glory. Oh, then there are the flowers with all their expanses of radiant color, creative shapes, and amazing fragrances.

Hiking trail, Frisco, Colorado

83

There are the millions of species of birds that have not a care as they fly with wings spread open, peacefully gliding on the air pockets of warm and cold currents.

And look at the spectacular animals that range from the smallest ant to the large, leathery, grey, massive elephant in Africa and India. Then there are the nations. We see the beauty of the Rift Valley in Kenya and the aurora lights in Alaska. I truly could go on and on, and those who know me know that I will. From seed-pods to seashells, carbon pressed rocks filled with glitter, to the light and fluffy multi-colored feathers of countless different birds—they cause me to *worship* God.

This is my Father's world.

## 8. Impressions from the Holy Spirit

These are gracious infiltrations into our spirit. When you get an impression from the Lord, you will know that it is from him. Ask God to confirm your intuition through scripture or others speaking into your life. You will also be led by the Holy Spirit if you are to speak up and share with others what you have learned from the Lord. It could be that your heart pounds and you know that you are to share scripture or a word that will encourage the body of Christ.

## 9. God's Will

We can trust God's nature and his perfect will for all things. God may communicate to us through his providential guidance through events that clearly reveal his will.

## 10. Burden-Bearer

> *Carry each other's burdens, and in this way you will fulfill the law of Christ.*
>
> —Gal. 6:2

There are some people who have an understanding and sensitivity for others with physical or emotional distress. Many call it the gift of mercy or burden-bearing (Rom. 12:3–6, 15).

The purpose of meditation, prayer, prophecy, healing, visions and dreams, God's Word, worship, and listening to God's voice is to reveal the glory of God to the human heart.

When it comes to the enchanting state of Colorado and its majestic mountains, I just can't get enough of them, looking at them from a distance and climbing them often. From the heights of the 14ers to the long and winding trails, I marvel at God's incredible handiwork as I strive to make it all the way to the top. Nothing can stop me as I rarely slow down to even catch my breath. I simply must stand in the clouds and oversee the rest of the surrounding mountains.

My husband and I recently hiked Mt. Evans on a cold and windy afternoon during the fall season. Mt. Evans is the highest summit of the Chicago Peaks in the front range of the Rocky Mountains in North America. In the fall months, we enjoy the acres and acres of glowing golden colors singing like aspen leaves dancing in the wind among the aspen trees.

Taking in all the scenery as we began driving up to experience a 14,000-foot mountain was absolutely breathtaking. The end of the tree line became more evident as we got higher up the mountain, and the crystal-clear blue lakes nestled in the valleys brought about a calming serenity to the picture-perfect day.

The narrow road taking us up to the parking area with no passing ability soon became dangerously steep and incredibly narrow with no guardrails. When I was in the passenger seat on the mountain side, I could look for miles ahead in great anticipation of our upcoming climb. But when I was on the cliff side with no guardrails, I became very nervous. The road that is so very far above sea level is the highest paved road you can drive on in North America. It was both breathtaking and life-shaking for me on that brisk, fall day.

Mt. Evans, Colorado

We arrived at the parking area and began the upward hike. We saw an Ebenezer as tall as I am. We then climbed true northward to make it to the summit. I remember making a statement to a stranger on the mountain about how overwhelmed I was with what God had created here on earth. He made the most profound comment: "Can you even begin to imagine what heaven will look like?" My heart was stirred with affection, joy, praise, and worship as I rose up to our God Most High on that hike. The Creator, the maker of heaven and earth, was on display for my enjoyment and for his glory on the mountain that fall day. As I worshipped with full abandonment on the mountain, I could hardly wait for the intense freedom we will have on *the* high places called heaven.

When we finished the hike and began our journey in the truck down the narrow road with no guardrails, I was overcome with an anxiety I had never before experienced. I had never in all my life experienced fear like this. I thought, *What has come over me, and why can't I trust my husband as he drives us down the narrow road with no guardrails?* I panicked, I cried, and I couldn't breathe. I was leaning all the way over to the driver's side trying not to look or be anywhere near the sharp drop-off. I wasn't afraid of dying, but the reality of possibly rolling down the mountain only to crash and burn freaked me out. My husband of 35 years had never seen me so scared. When we were finally back in the foothills filled with evergreen trees and wildflowers, I began to weep. My emotions took a 180-degree turn from the overwhelming fear to the peace of an ever-present faith and freedom in the Holy Spirit. An enormous sense of joy, gratitude, and deep worship came over me like a flood. I experienced God in the most profound way that late afternoon. He allowed and even entrusted me with a range of deep emotions in my heart that day. That emotion caused me to rely on him and experience him from the depths of my innermost being. Experiencing him is dangerously sweet.

## When Your Ears Are Open

*Whoever has ears, let them hear what the Spirit says to the churches.*
—Rev. 2:11

It is doubtful that you will hear God's voice if you don't believe he is speaking. But you never know—he spoke through an ass (donkey) when he needed to (Num. 22:21–41).

God speaks to those who listen.

God is more concerned with the depth of your commitment to him than all your accolades and busyness for him.

God is quick to speak to those who are quick to obey.

The humble in heart hears his voice.

The proud want their own way; the humble in heart want God's way.

Psalm 25:9; Isaiah 57:15, 66:1–2; James 4:6; 1 Peter 5:5–6; Numbers 12:1

Be alone with God, away from others.

Be silent before the Lord. Sit and meditate on the Word of God. "I will consider all your works and meditate on all your mighty deeds" (Ps. 77:12). (Also see Josh. 1:8, Ps. 119: 97–100, Ps. 143:5.)

Be patient. "Yes, my soul, find rest in God; my hope comes from him" (Ps. 62:5).

Be confident in the Lord. "For the LORD will be at your side and will keep your foot from being snared" (Prov. 3:26). (Also see Luke 11:5–13.)

Be regular in your time meeting God to pray and meditate. Make meditation a habit, and be persistent in listening to God.

As you pray and meditate before the Lord, ask God, "What do you want to say to me through the Bible? What do you want to say to my heart right now as I think on you?"

If God gives you an encouraging word to share with someone in the body, it will always be for building up the individual and the church, never to tear down or bring about division.

## Posture Matters

> *That which was from the beginning, which we have heard, which we have seen with our eyes, which we have looked at and our hands have touched—this we proclaim concerning the Word of life.*
>
> —1 John 1:1

*Standing:*

> *And the Levites—Jeshua, Kadmiel, Bani, Hashabneiah, Sherebiah, Hodiah, Shebaniah and Pethahiah—said: "Stand up and praise the LORD your God, who is from everlasting to everlasting."*
>
> *"Blessed be your glorious name, and may it be exalted above all blessing and praise."*
>
> —Neh. 9:5

*Hands Lifted:*

> *Therefore I want the men everywhere to pray, lifting up holy hands without anger or disputing.*
>
> —1 Tim. 2:8

*Kneeling:*

> *Then, at evening sacrifice, I rose from my self-abasement, with my tunic and cloak torn, and fell on my knees with my hands spread out to the LORD my God.*
>
> —Ezra 9:5

*Bowing:*

> *Moses bowed to the ground at once and worshiped.*
>
> —Exod. 34:8

*Sitting:*

> *Then King David went in and sat before the LORD, and he said: "Who am I, Sovereign LORD, and what is my family, that you have brought me this far?*
>
> —2 Sam. 7:18

Throughout the Bible, from Genesis to the maps (I hope you have maps in your Bible), we read that men and women prayed everywhere, from the valleys to the mountaintops. In the book of Acts, we read where prayer meetings took place.

- In the upper room – Acts 1:13–14
- In a home – Acts 12:5
- By a river – Acts 16:13
- On a beach – Acts 21:5

We read in the New Testament that we are to pray:

- In secret – Matthew 6:6
- With family – Acts 10:2–3
- In a group – Matthew 18:20
- In public – 1 Corinthians 14:14–17

## Praying God's Word

> *All Scripture is God-breathed and is useful for teaching, rebuking, correcting and training in righteousness.*
>
> —2 Tim. 3:16

Praying scripture is as easy as it sounds. Choose a passage, and pray it back to God. If you are going through a difficult time, find scripture for that situation, and pray it back to God. The same applies for the blessings in our lives. Let's look at some examples of how to entreat the written words of God.

In 1 Samuel 12:18–25, we see that the people wanted Samuel to pray to God on their behalf. They had done many evil things before the Lord and needed to repent. Samuel tells the people to not be afraid and to repent, to turn away from their sins. He wanted to encourage them to serve God with all their hearts. Samuel prayed for the people and then declared, "I will teach you the way that is good and right" (1 Sam. 12:23). Using 1 Samuel 12:24, we can pray scripture something like this: Help me to fear you, Lord, and serve you faithfully with all my heart; may I consider what great things you have done for me.

Today, we don't need a high priest to intercede on our behalf. We can go straight to the Father and pray. We have full access to the throne of grace by the blood of the Lamb, Jesus. Praise the Lord! Hallelujah! (Heb. 4:14–16). I suggest being in a quiet place when you pray scripture.

Here's another way to pray scripture using Philippians 3:10–11, for example: I want to know Christ and the power of his resurrection and the fellowship of sharing in his sufferings, becoming like him in his death, and so, somehow, to attain to the resurrection from the dead. In Jesus's name, amen.

Coming to a deep understanding of what Jesus did on the cross through obedience and a love for all humanity is both spectacular and majestic. It is in Christ's resurrection that we are to fully realize God's might and power. We can't obtain that perfection this side of heaven, but we sure can strive toward the mark of his high calling through Christ Jesus. God has called us to have heavenward prayers.

> *Rejoice in the Lord always. I will say it again: Rejoice! Let your gentleness be evident to all. The Lord is near. Do not be anxious about anything, but in every situation, by prayer and petition, with thanksgiving, present your requests to God. And the peace of God, which transcends all understanding, will guard your hearts and your minds in Christ Jesus.*
>
> *Finally, brothers and sisters, whatever is true, whatever is noble, whatever is right, whatever is pure, whatever is lovely, whatever is admirable—if anything is excellent or praiseworthy—think about such things. Whatever you have learned or received or heard from me, or seen in me—put it into practice. And the God of peace will be with you.*
>
> —Phil. 4:4–9

As a certified biblical counselor, I meet with many young women who struggle with gripping anxiety. The Lord has giving me love, caring, and understanding that comes from the Holy Spirit to listen, pray, and counsel them toward truth. The fact is that most Christians don't take God's Word as absolute reality. I wrestle with my flesh, my pride, and my selfishness, placing my feelings over the legitimacy of God's written Word. We must take him at his Word, for it will not return void. Praying truly calms the soul, spirit, and mind. Pray often.

Philippians 4:4–9 has rocked my heart as I have put these words under a microscope, meditated on the passage, and allowed it to take root in my mind. Something beautiful dropped in my spirit when I came to grips with the fact that the Lord is near and that I can rejoice in my salvation.

When I am tender and calm and display God's love to others, God is near. *The Lord is near!* Then the very next statement is, "Do not be anxious about anything, but in every situation, by prayer and petition, with thanksgiving, present your requests to God" (Phil. 4:6). Make your appeal to God. Your request must be made with thanksgiving. Well, that's a tough pill to swallow sometimes.

Let's look more closely at how to rejoice, be kind, and in thanksgiving make your needs known to God so we can feel God's nearness. He is already near to you, but now you can feel his presence upon you.

God is intimately acquainted with us. He knows the number of hairs on our head and knows what is in our hearts. So we might as well be completely honest with God and bare our souls before him. Let those anxieties that flood your innermost being come up and out. Out of your mouth, your heart speaks. There is something freeing about speaking out loud to God all your heartaches and pains.

Now, thank God for the gift of what he is allowing you to experience, even the most difficult of situations. He was a man of many sorrows, acquainted with grief. Jesus bears your burdens.

God doesn't leave us hanging. He instructs us to think about whatever is true, noble, right, pure, lovely, and admirable. And if anything is excellent or praiseworthy, we are to think about such things.

When you put it into practice (God knows it takes time and practice), you will have peace—God's peace that surpasses all understanding and guards your heart in Christ Jesus.

It is hard to walk in the spirit at all times. We get distracted and busy and selfish. We can think on these things.

*I want to know Christ—yes, to know the power of his resurrection and participation in his sufferings, becoming like him in his death, and so, somehow, attaining to the resurrection from the dead.*

*Not that I have already obtained all this, or have already arrived at my goal, but I press on to take hold of that for which Christ Jesus took hold of me. Brothers and sisters, I do not consider myself yet to have taken hold of it. But one thing I do: Forgetting what is behind and straining toward what is ahead, I press on toward the goal to win the prize for which God has called me heavenward in Christ Jesus.*

—Phil. 3:10–14

## How to Pray for . . .

Praying salvation for a family member or a friend can indeed become a labor. There are people who are recipients of more than 30 years of personal intercession on their behalf. So let us pray God's very words back to him because God's Word brings life and truth.

*Salvation*

Dear Lord, I lift up John that he would confess with his mouth Jesus as Lord and believe in his heart that God raised Jesus from the dead. I pray this so that John will be saved (Rom. 10:9).

*Healing*

Lord I lift up my dear friend Susan. I pray that she may enjoy good health and that all may go well with her, even as her soul is being tested (3 John 2).

*Our pastors and those in leadership*

Lord, I lift up our church, our pastors, and their families in prayer. Place them in the shelter of God Most High to rest in the shadow of the Almighty. I will say to the Lord, you are their refuge and fortress. I pray you will preserve their family time and that your faithfulness will meet their financial needs in Christ Jesus (Phil. 4:19).

*Our government*

Thank you, Lord, that we have the privilege of interceding for our leaders. You urge us to let our requests, prayers, intercessions, and thanksgiving be made known for everyone, for kings and all those in authority, that we may live peacefully and have quiet lives in all godliness and holiness. This is good and pleasing unto you (1 Tim. 2:1–2).

*Ourselves*

Dear Lord, help me trust in you with all my heart and lean not on my own understanding but in all ways acknowledge you, and you will direct my path (Prov. 3:5–6).

## Blessing the Lord

*Praise the LORD, my soul.*

*LORD my God, you are very great;*
*you are clothed with splendor and majesty.*

—Ps. 104:1

## Psalms

*I will sing to the LORD,*
*for he is highly exalted.*

—Exod. 15:1

There are 150 beautifully composed psalms of poetry in the book of Psalms. David, Moses, Asaph (David's worship leader), Korah (from the Levite family), Orphans (possible from tradition), and several minor contributors such as Solomon, Ethan, and Heman added to this poetic section in the Bible.

As you daily read through the passages in Psalms, highlight the character and attributes of God. For instance, in Psalm 28, highlight the words *rock, strength, fortress of salvation,* and *shepherd.* This is who God is in that chapter. Once you have read the entire book of Psalms and highlighted it with God's character and attributes, you will see who God is in a brighter way. Who God is will be jumping off the pages as you read the book of Psalms. You will forever see those highlighted words as you open those pages. Pray the Psalms. Pray scripture in the Bible.

*To you, Lord, I call; you are my Rock,*
  *do not turn a deaf ear to me.*
*For if you remain silent,*
  *I will be like those who go down to the pit.*
*Hear my cry for mercy as I call to you for help,*
  *as I lift up my hands toward your Most Holy Place.*

*Do not drag me away with the wicked,*
  *with those who do evil,*
*who speak cordially with their neighbors*
  *but harbor malice in their hearts.*
*Repay them for their deeds*
  *and for their evil work;*
*repay them for what their hands have done*
  *and bring back on them what they deserve.*

*Because they have no regard for the deeds of the Lord*
  *and what his hands have done,*
*he will tear them down*
  *and never build them up again.*

*Praise be to the Lord,*
  *for he has heard my cry for mercy.*
*The Lord is my strength and my shield;*
  *my heart trusts in him, and he helps me.*
*My heart leaps for joy,*
  *and with my song I praise him.*

*The Lord is the strength of his people,*
  *a fortress of salvation for his anointed one.*
*Save your people and bless your inheritance;*
  *be their shepherd and carry them forever.*

—Ps. 28:1–9

The day after my dad's funeral, I could not even read my Bible or pray. I was numb. I sat in my comfortable chair and began my TAG

(Time Alone with God). All I could do was weep. My eyes were closed, and my heart was very heavy; I encountered a vision of my dad walking with Jesus.

God allowed me to see my dad and Jesus together as they walked through a beautiful, lush garden. They walked side-by-side with one another and talked. My dad had made some major mistakes that led to sin against God, himself, and my mom. He had left her after almost 40 years of marriage. My dad was weeping as he walked with Jesus in the garden.

Jesus's head turned toward my dad, and he asked my dad a very simple yet profound question.

"Why did you turn to the world when you had me?"

I often ask myself that question.

My earthly father sobbed before the Lord and profoundly stated that he was so sorry. Jesus smiled and said, "It's been paid for."

When the vision was over, I opened my Bible to the book of Psalms, and all I could do was read the highlighted words and phrases. It turned into worship. It turned into healing of the soul, worship through his poetry in the book of Psalms.

Pray as you read through the Word, pray when you close the good book to begin your day, and continue to seek his face all day long. Precept Bible studies uses the inductive method in studying God's Word. It is one of the deepest, most life-changing Bible studies available.

As you read through the Psalms, praying those passages back to God, his Word will come alive with raw outpourings of those saints and prophets who wrote the book.

You will experience God in your heart as you pour out your life before him. Reading through the book of Psalms and praying those words back to God pleases him. The Bible is God's words, and God loves his words spoken in prayer back to him.

I want to encourage my poets, artists, and songwriter friends to write and illustrate your prayers to God. Sing your own songs of praise, and lament and weep as your songs of lament from your soul in times of trouble are lifted up to God. Before you know it, you will have a collection of praises to your Lord and Savior.

## Life Scriptures

> *I have hidden your word in my heart that I might not sin against you.*
>
> —Ps. 119:11

If you have ever been rock climbing, you know that safety is key for a successful climb. I'll never forget my first rappelling experience and what I learned before I did it. You put the climbing rope through the carabiner in a Munter hitch or Prusik knot to descend the mountain. Make sure to listen for the sound of the click as the carabiner locks in place. That ensures that the rope is safely in place and you are ready to rappel down from the top of the mountain.

You wear a harness that wraps around your legs and waist, strapping you in with the rope secure in your hands. At the top of the mountain is where the rope is anchored; it is the greatest point of security for the climber. This secure point on either the top of a mountain or on a side of a mountain prepares you to go down in almost a sudden vertical drop.

*Belay* is a word that a climber calls out from the top of the mountain to the person below. With a listening ear, you long to hear "belay on" from the person at the bottom of the mountain, confirming that it's time to step back, descend, and trust that they have you securely in their hands with the dangling rope.

You take in a deep breath and pray a strong faith-based prayer as you lean back and make your first maneuver into what feels like stepping into midair.

Your hands covered with thick leather gloves are tightly grasping the rope with every fiber of your being. Once again, you find yourself praying that the rope will not only hold your weight but also securely bring you safely down the mountain.

Having the security of hearing the carabiner click into place is not only a comforting sound, but it also gives a feeling of confidence and safety. The same applies with hiding God's Word in your heart.

God's Word gives you confidence and safety when you are facing difficult times in your life or even needing to have a secure, stable mindset about life. Having a life scripture is essential. When you secure a scrip-

Lusaka, Zambia, Africa

ture in your heart, it brings about a safe and assuring anchor throughout your life.

A life scripture is a verse, verses, or maybe even a full chapter of the Bible that you memorize, and it naturally comes to the forefront of your heart when you need peace and assurance that God is in control of your situation.

I recall hiding two scriptures in my heart when I was very young. I didn't go through anything particularly difficult, yet these scriptures spoke to me in a meaningful way. I relied on them for comfort and truth. I still run to those verses all the time and have added several more life scriptures over the years.

> *Trust in the Lord with all your heart*
> *and lean not on your own understanding;*
> *in all your ways submit to him,*
> *and he will make your paths straight.*
>
> —Prov. 3:5–6

In the original Hebrew language, the scripture reads something like this: Trust in the Lord (what do you need from me, Lord?). I trust you with all my heart. I am to lean on you. In all my ways I am to know you intimately. Jesus, you are our way and the path to God, but what do you need from me?

When we arrive at the heavenly gates, only love will prevail for an unending time. We will no longer need faith or hope.

God's heart is the greatest exploration you will ever know. Come to know him right now. Knowing God's Word is truth, but it is also fully coming to know God himself. Come to know God.

There are four letters in the Hebrew word for *now*.

Reading from right to left in the Hebrew alphabet:

## עכשיו
## NOW

Crucified one / consummation / crown / glory / to see and to understand (right to left)

Hebrew helps us see and understand that Jesus is crowned in glory, the consummation of all things, the crucified one. See him in truth with Hebrew eyes. Let's not just read the Word of God; let's walk in it. It is a living language; it is alive *now*.

> *And we know that in all things God works for the good of those who love him, who have been called according to his purpose. For those God foreknew, he also predestined to be conformed to the image of his Son.*
>
> —Rom. 8:28–29

Holding these life scriptures secure in our hearts and minds will assist us throughout life, from the challenging times to simply desiring to worship God with his own beautiful words. We know that God's Word will not return void. Whatever you behold, you become.

John Piper said it perfectly in his book *Let the Nations Be Glad*. "God is most glorified in us when we are most satisfied in Him."[2]

The memorization of scripture is like a carabiner. As we speak God's Word out loud or in our hearts, we are confident that God is near and has us in the palm of his hand.

---

2. John Piper, *Let the Nations Be Glad* (Grand Rapids, MI: Baker Books, 1993).

The solid foundation of God's Word hidden in our heart helps us fight sin. The firm foundation is the rock of strength, peace, assurance, and love. God is near. The rock at the top of the mountain is where we run when we need solace (Ps. 121).

We have a natural bent to rely on self and sometimes counsel from others and the world. As followers of Christ, we truly know that God's Word brings the ultimate peace and comfort. We have been given the sweetest gift of the Holy Spirit to guide us in all truth. Therefore, let us run to God, His Word, and prayer with the help of the Holy Spirit to lead us on the climb called life.

The three strands of a rope is the Word of God, Jesus, and the Holy Spirit shed abroad in our hearts through Christ Jesus.

We have safety and security in Christ alone as we cling to the three strands woven together.

The memorized Word of God in your heart will at times be used in ministry to others by speaking love and truth when they need counsel from God's Word.

As we cry out "Belay," indicating we're ready to come down the mountain, may we hear from our reliable instructor, "Belay on!"

God is our rock, our sure foundation. Jesus and His Word are the security of our lifeline. Our very cornerstone, our instructor, is waiting for us to call upon him for guidance, counsel, assurance, and wisdom. He will indeed instruct and rebuke us when needed. This is the gift of the Holy Spirit as we go through life.

When we cry out "Belay," God's response is this: "Come on! I've got you. Belay on. You are secure in my Word and in me."

## Fasting

> "Even now," declares the LORD [Adonai – Lord and Master],
> "return to me with all your heart,
> with fasting and weeping and mourning."

> Rent your heart
> and not your garments.

*Return to the LORD your God,*
*for he is gracious and compassionate,*
*slow to anger and abounding in love,*
*and relents from sending calamity.*

—Joel 2:12–13

To rend your heart is to tear away from your sin nature. Your heart is the seat of all things—your breath (your words), mind, spirit, and soul. Our hearts are wicked above all else, yet they can be turned from stone into hearts of flesh when we get in step with the Spirit.

The Israelites would tear their garments in the assembly to show an outward sign of sorrow, shame, and a repentant heart for their sins. That was a public testament before God and their peers that they were humbling themselves. They would throw dirt upon their heads and weep loudly, mourn, wail, and lament.

Today, we can confess our sins one to another so we might be healed in Jesus's name.

Lord, fillet our hearts and cut out the sin that is ever before us. Clean us and wash us, allowing our hearts to be completely led by the unction of the Holy Spirit (James 5:16).

Fasting, weeping, and mourning are outward signs of a heart that desires to confess, repent, and walk in a manner worthy of God's great mercy. The real work is done inside our minds, souls, spirits, and hearts. When we become a people who are stained by Jesus's blood and marked by the sign of the cross, that's what reflects his glory and grace upon us as followers of the Way.

In Matthew 6:16, we read that Jesus stated, "When you fast." Jesus is expecting us to set aside time away from the table and spend time alone with him, abiding in his love.

Prayer, reading the Bible, worshiping him, enjoying and delighting in him—that is what replaces food, binging on TV, and social media for a day or a season. Fasting is a break so you refocus on godly things.

So why do we need to abstain?

We need to cut away from our schedule and replace food with maybe freedom in the presence of the Lord.

We need to refrain from social media and focus on the true scroll, God's written Word. There's no need to be legalistic; this is a private time between you and the Lord.

You will know in and out of season when to set aside more time alone with God (TAG). We abstain to gain. We step out of the world and into his realm. Why do we hesitate? He has so much to teach us, and I say let's learn all we can on this side of heaven.

When you are led by the Holy Spirit to go before the Lord and rend your heart, soon you will begin to taste and see the sweet joy of his intimacy on a very deep level.

The caution is not to make fasting a repetition of the law but to indeed earnestly seek God's face—to see that he is gracious, compassionate, slow to anger, and abounding in love. His will for us is not calamity but order. Yet, my dear friend, he just might ask you to fast weekly to get more of him in a special time of setting aside other things for time alone with God.

We fast to replace food or social media in our daily routine of life, to use that time wisely to pray, worship, and study God's Word more intensely. It can also be a time of serving others, looking outward versus inward navel-gazing.

The discipline of refraining from food or social media is so our minds will be focused on God, his Word, and his ways. We must desire to seek God with all our heart, soul, and strength, to seek him and find him. Fasting can also be a discipline of not spending frivolously or partaking in wine or beer in excess or (fill in the blanks). Just ask. He will prompt you in your journey of fasting.

Fasting can lend itself to bring about a time of instruction from the Holy Spirit. These precepts and this discipline can lead you to be more fluid as you learn hidden truths through God's Word. I call these seeds of righteousness ahas or oy veys, depending on the lesson learned.

This mandate of cleansing your heart will train you to hear God more distinctively. I suggest praying alone and asking for clear direction before you start your fasting period.

When you read the Bible, it is full of instructions and warnings. Listen up! He is speaking to you. Are you hearing his voice in your heart, soul, and mind? God disciplines those he loves.

There is a picture of our lead pastor, Matt Chandler of The Village Church (TVC), that is forever ingrained in my memory. In a dream I had, Matt is surrounded by great men of astounding faith. These men are standing on the stairs leading into the entrance of the sanctuary at the Dallas TVC. Matt is standing right in the middle of these men who have bowed heads and outstretched hands toward him, praying for their brother and asking God to heal him by the authority of Jesus's name. Matt holds his hands together near his mouth in the position of prayer, and today you will see that very depiction in a photo in his office.

This vision of his deeply scarred, bald, and bowed head in prayer with strong men of faith by his side is encouraging. We must follow the mandate to intercede for one another and lift each other up with prayer and fasting.

When I awoke, the Lord gave me an unwavering belief that Matt would be healed of his brain tumor. The day I read the staff email of his surgery, I spoke out loud, "Lord, this is Matt Chandler." And as I was closing my computer, the Lord spoke to my heart and said, "Yes, I know." Right then I knew. I cannot explain it; I just knew that Matt would be healed by God for the world to see God's glory.

My husband, Mark, and I have set our phone alarms for 8:30 p.m. for years, and no matter where we are, we stop to pray for Matt's healing. To this day, we still pray for him and his family when led by the Holy Spirit.

Mark and I have experienced the sweet joy of praying for Matt daily. We have entered into the presence of the Lord in order to stand in the gap for this gifted young pastor, husband, and father. It also was a great witnessing tool without us ever intending it to be. We stopped to pray in restaurants, family gatherings, movie theaters, events, and even in church to intercede for Matt during his dark night of the soul. Sometimes, people asked us what we were doing, and we were able to share with them the good news of Christ.

Matt Chandler has been healed from oligodendroglioma brain cancer. God receives all the glory, honor, and praise. What's really crazy is that I had that dream of those godly men praying for Matt before he came out of the hospital. I was overwhelmed with an assurance of healing for God to be high and lifted up. I knew that his miraculous healing would reach the nations for God's ultimate honor and glory.

Matt's cancer was not without great pain, anguish, and suffering. It was a deep, perceived shift in his life, an interruption that caused him to dive deeper into scripture, prayer, and the Holy Spirit to help him walk through depression. Matt's life hung in the balance for a long time, yet he clung to Jesus for his comfort.

God will do what he chooses to do for his glory. Matt Chandler is president of the Acts 29 ministries nationwide, and everyone knows his story of faith during the fight. Acts 29 is a diverse, global family of church-planting churches everywhere to see the gospel go forth and for all people to come to saving grace through Jesus Christ.

Does everyone we pray for get healed the way we desire? No, but we can pray for the end goal, which is to be spiritually healed, to know God and make him known, no matter our lot in life. It is well with my soul.

As we focus on what Christ's body endured on the cross and that his blood poured out was for our transgressions, then we remember, we mourn, and we rejoice. The mixture of sorrow and joy and remembering all that Christ accomplished on the cross is for the redemption of people. It was finished, yet it will not be completed until his return and there is a gathering of the saints. Blood and water flowed down the cross as a sign of a broken heart.

The most important thing to recognize is that the sole purpose of fasting is to adjust our hearts to be in tune with God's heart. It is good to intercede for a specific need or request before the Lord. Can the Lord do whatever he pleases? Yes, and he allows us to join him in the process so we experience his great love.

During your time of fasting and prayer, you can enter the very throne room of heaven and make your requests known to God.

## Intercession

*But when you pray, go into your room, close the door and pray to your Father, who is unseen. Then your Father, who sees what is done in secret, will reward you.*

—Matt. 6:6

Private intercessory prayer is a force to be reckoned with. When it's just you and the Father, much work can be accomplished through quiet submission. As you are listening to his voice as you cry out to God, you will sense that he is near. When you spend hours before the King in prayer and then close in the name of Jesus, you will be filled with tranquility in every fiber of your being.

You have done business with the Almighty King as you have laid your requests before him. He longs to hear your voice, and he longs to speak to you. Jehovah Raah, the Lord is our Shepherd, is leading us into the way of everlasting joy. God's sheep know his sound and desire to follow him. The key is listening to him through his Word and his still, small voice within your innermost being. Meditating on the cross and God's Word will align your heart to see him.

I also want to encourage those who do not like to pray out loud in a group. That is okay. Maybe you are shy or uncomfortable in a group setting. I want to spur you on to listen to the prayer requests, agree with those petitions that have been made, and pray in your spirit for those you are with.

One of the sweetest memories of a short prayer was at a student gathering in our home. A young girl was requesting prayer after a time of extended worship, so we gathered around her to lay hands on her and pray. Everyone had lifted up their voices in prayer on her behalf, yet one teenager was quiet. Then, out of the quiet young man's heart, he said, "God, thank you for Jenny." It was a sweet, genuine, earnest blessing for her. The prayer was heartfelt and prayed in humility. We all felt the grave importance of life—it's a gift. Jenny is a gift to the body. We are all loved, valued, and have purpose. A simple thanks to God goes a long way.

I believe that everyone in the room that night felt the power of the Holy Spirit in that moment. We ended the gathering that evening knowing we had experienced God's grace on us all.

Prayers do not need to be lengthy; they only need to come from your heart. There are no wrong or silly prayers as you speak to your Lord. Scripture tells us that if we pray silly prayers, the Holy Spirit will intercede for us.

God loves it when you talk to him. God will use you to uplift another in need as you stand in the gap on their behalf. Be encouraged.

# Meditation

## Prayers Hindered

*We know that God does not listen to sinners. He listens to the godly person who does his will.*

—John 9:31

Lack of Love – Luke 6:38, Proverbs 21:13, 17:9
Pride and Selfishness – James 4:3
Unbelief and Doubt – Hebrews 11:6, James 1:5–8
Disobedience – Proverbs 10:24, 1 John 3:21–22
Family Discord and Strife – 1 Peter 3:7
Unforgiveness – Matthew 6:12–15
Lack of Reconciliation – Matthew 5:23–24
Unconfessed Sin – Psalm 66:18, Isaiah 59:1–2
Religion and Idolatry – Hosea 5
When Not in God's Will – 1 John 5:14

God has a perfect will and plan for your life. He also has a permissive will, allowing you to have free will.

*Husbands, in the same way be considerate as you live with your wives, and treat them with respect as the weaker partner and as heirs with you of the gracious gift of life, so that nothing will hinder your prayers.*

—1 Pet. 3:7

*Whoever would love life and see good days must keep their tongue from evil and their lips from deceitful speech. They must turn from evil and do good; they must seek peace and pursue it. For the eyes of the Lord are on the righteous and his ears are attentive to their prayer, but the face of the Lord is against those who do evil.*

—1 Pet. 3:10–12

God shows us a way to live before him in his presence. He wants us to obey his written Word and live a life set apart from the world's deceptiveness. He calls us to be holy as he is holy, desiring for us to live a life of integrity and moral righteousness before him. When we can uphold God's Word, it enhances our prayer life as we see him as King and Lord over all our situations. We are to have sound judgment in all issues of life so we can walk in forgiveness since unforgiveness hinders our prayers. As followers of Christ, we are to be sober-minded and confess our sins one to another so we can be set free from the bondage of sin.

Being vulnerable and organic with one another is messy and beautiful at the same time.

Walking in love and authenticity toward one another will sharpen us to be more like Christ. If you hold unconfessed sin in your soul, you will suffer one way or another. Destruction is a high price to pay for hidden sin.

## Silence

*I meditate on your precepts and consider your ways.*

—Ps. 119:15

The definition of meditation includes contemplation, thought, thinking, pondering, consideration, reflection, deliberation, rumination, and concentration. It is a written or spoken conversation expressing thoughts on a subject. Meditation is engaging in a mental exercise in order to reach spiritual awareness.

In Hebrew, there are two words for meditation:

*Haga* – to sigh or murmur

*Siha* – to muse or rehearse in one's mind. Think about these meanings
  as you read this passage.

> *Blessed is the one*
> > *who does not walk in step with the wicked*
> *or stand in the way that sinners take*
> > *or sit in the company of mockers,*
> *but whose delight is in the law of the* Lord,
> > *and who meditates on his law day and night.*
> *That person is like a tree planted by streams of water,*
> > *which yields its fruit in season*
> *and whose leaf does not wither—*
> > *whatever they do prospers.*
>
> *Not so the wicked!*
> > *They are like chaff that the wind blows away.*
> *Therefore the wicked will not stand in the judgment,*
> > *nor sinners in the assembly of the righteous.*
>
> *For the* Lord *watches over the way of the righteous,*
> > *but the way of the wicked leads to destruction.*
>
> —Ps. 1:1–6

Thinking deeply upon the Lord and reflecting on his Word for a long period of time is a discipline most do not engage in. We are to delight in the law of the Lord and meditate on it day and night.

Life can get in the way, and yet this is where we draw our strength—from God's Word and our intimate relationship with him. How we treat people and interact with them is evidence of our true religion—a relationship. I always say how we worship on a Sunday should be a reflection of our week we had with God.

Boy's rescue home, Rift Valley, Kenya, Africa

When we find ourselves dry and without passion in our TAG, not having vision or clarity for our lives, it just might be time to stop and sit before the Lord. In fact, you know it's time because we are to enter in daily with the Lord through the Holy Spirit. David went into the sanctuary; he entered with humility as he sat before the Lord and asked this:

> *Who am I, Sovereign* Lord, *and what is my family, that you have brought me this far?*
>
> —2 Sam. 7:18

David feared God. The translation of the word *fear* in this passage means to worship God with great awe. Let us come and worship the Lord with a holy fear and reverence. Let us bow before him in adoration, praise, and thanksgiving, for he is good, and his love endures forever.

## From the Heart

> *Tremble and do not sin; when you are on your beds,*
> *search your hearts and be silent.*
>
> —Ps. 4:4

> *May my meditation be pleasing to him,*
> *as I rejoice in the* Lord.
>
> —Ps. 104:34

When we set aside time and space to be engulfed in God's presence, we will hear from him. I suggest praying with your heart and mind focused on Christ. You will engage in a more meaningful time as you embark on contemplating God and scripture. There is something about focusing on the cross that sets the tone for worship, prayer, and reflection on God.

Keep in mind that the enemy imitates God's design and his ways. I know that some might read about how to meditate on the Lord and think that it is New Age. Reflecting on God and his Word is the authentic structure for truth. Christianity is an Eastern religion that instituted concentrating on the Lord and his ways. All the other religions imitate and misuse the true source of its foundation—God himself and his precepts.

When believers meditate, the focus is on God, Jesus, the Holy Spirit, and God's Word. We have the mind of Christ due to the words of Christ. We have the guaranteed deposit of the Holy Spirit within us, and he leads us in all truth. It's not a formula; it's freedom. Trust God and his Word. Trust the Holy Spirit who is at work to teach us all things (John 14:26, Matt. 28:18–20).

The Holy Spirit teaches us about Jesus (John 16:12–14).

The Holy Spirit comforts us and gives us strength to fight sin (Acts 1:5–8, Eph. 4:30, Gal. 5:16–25).

The Holy Spirit is our Counselor (John 16:16, 25).

The Holy Spirit never leaves us (John 16:18).

The Holy Spirit prays for us when we don't know how to pray (Rom. 8:23).

The Holy Spirit guides us in all truth (John 16:13).

The Holy Spirit is peace (John 16:27).

The Holy Spirit testifies with our spirit that we are children of God (Rom. 8:16).

The precepts of God are weighed, and the plumb line is his Word:

*Hear, O Israel: The LORD our God, the LORD is one. Love the LORD your God with all your heart and with all your soul and with all your strength.*

—Deut. 6:4–5

When we become a body of believers that truly loves God with all our heart, soul, and strength, think how different we would be personally.

What would our churches look like with this amazing crazy love? Love can transform our families and our world by God's love.

Meditation and prayer have the mind descending down into the heart. Meditation ignites us to love God's Word as we are required to pray and meditate on the Lord.

Godly meditation fills our minds with God, and the same happens when we pray in our spiritual prayer language. Remember, this is a gift you can ask for.

Tucker Cabin, Frisco, Colorado

## Attentive

> *My son, pay attention to what I say;*
> *turn your ear to my words.*
> *Do not let them out of your sight,*
> *keep them within your heart;*
> *for they are life to those who find them*
> *and health to one's whole body.*
>
> —Prov. 4:20–22

> *May these words of my mouth and this meditation of my heart*
> *be acceptable in your sight,*
> *LORD, my Rock and my Redeemer.*
>
> —Ps. 19:14

It's a peaceful morning, and no one else is up yet, maybe not even the sun. You grab your Bible and sit in your comfortable chair in a quiet, formal living room or a cozy den. It's your place of prayer. You grab a warm blanket, wrap it around you during the cold of winter, and have a hot cup of your favorite beverage sitting on your side table.

You open the logos and ask the Holy Spirit to lead you in all truth as you begin to read. You whisper, "Come, Holy Spirit, come" from your lips. Maybe you are reading systematically through the Bible or you are in a particular book in the Bible. Today, your TAG might be simply meditating on a few passages. As you begin journaling what your heart caught from the Rhema of the Word, you begin to experience God's Word in a new way. He is near and real to you.

Your daily devotional book has just inspired you to stop and reflect on a particularly powerful passage. Your mind needs to contemplate all you have just experienced. Here we go—time to close your eyes and pray. Out of the overflow of your heart comes a great thankfulness to God for his supernatural kindness to you.

Praising God for who he is and thinking on him, you begin to be keenly aware of his presence. Rest in his comfort. His word is active and sharper than any two-edged sword.

One way to meditate is to go over a passage or verse several times. Read at a normal pace at first, and then slow down as you reread it. Now read a word at a time, as each word has new meaning and substance to it. You might begin to envision something in your mind's eye as your head is bowed and eyes shut.

Ask God to speak to you through his Word. Listen, relax, and rely on the Holy Spirit to reveal to you what God is longing to say to you through the Word, a vision, or a dream.

It's that small, still voice that you know deep in your spirit that bears witness with you. He is the good Shepherd, and you know his voice. There is no doubt about his authority.

God has given us all gifts that build up the body of his church. Your gift will be different from others in your circle of family, friends, and community. That's good news because we want to be diverse people to accomplish his will here on earth with the gifts given to us.

If you have visions or dreams, meditation can often bring about these events. The Bible instructs us that the gifts are for building up the body as we encourage one another. The more you are engulfed by the very presence of God, the stronger your intimacy will grow in him. The more you spend time with him, the greater your gifting increases.

Write down the vision or dream. When the vision or dream occurs and you don't have your journal or device nearby to record it, you will not forget it the next time. When a vision or dream is from the Lord, you will recall every detail.

The same principle applies when you hear that small, still voice giving you a word for someone. Always test it to see whether it's from God or whether it's a thought in your head. I personally take a few weeks of praying before I say anything to my brother or sister about the word or vision I had about them. I even tell them, "I sense that the Lord has impressed something on my heart for you to be encouraged."

There are also times when God speaks to you on the spot, no matter where you are, and you will know that it is his voice you hear and that you need to obey him. It can be in an instant, and that's when you trust God, listen, and wait for further instructions.

We have dear friends who were in the process of adopting a baby. The money was raised quickly as many people wanted to support this amazing godly couple. On a Sunday evening after the church service, I asked the wife how things were going. She was so thrilled to share that they got news of a teenage mom who chose them to adopt her unborn baby. We celebrated together since they had been waiting for a very long time for a match. As she began telling me this great news, out of my mouth came an odd question. "Is the baby biracial?" To be honest, I thought, why did I just ask that? She shared that the baby's biological parents were of the same race.

Immediately, the Lord spoke in my heart and mind and said (almost loudly), "That's not their baby." Say what? I said nothing to her, but apparently the demeanor on my face changed in that moment.

On the drive home from church that night, she told her husband about our conversation. She shared with him that she didn't think I was excited for them as the expression on my face changed as she began to share the details of the parents.

Immediately, I took to prayer, and for the next several weeks, I asked God to give me the right opportunity to talk to my young pastor friend. I asked the Holy Spirit to lead me when to share with him if, indeed, that was God's will. How would this word encourage them?

The time came when I found myself in front of my brother in Christ. I humbly stated that I had something to share after spending weeks in prayer. We know this young man well. He was in our home group and is like a son to us. I wasn't nervous as I shared what the Lord spoke to me about their adoption process; nevertheless, I relied heavily on the Spirit to speak through me.

He looked at me in the most unusual way as I spoke of what the Lord had said to me about the adoption. He began to share that they were not going to get to adopt the baby promised to them. He stated that hearing how the Lord spoke to me encouraged him that indeed there was a right baby to be placed in their lives. He saw the good in the message.

Now, they have the most beautiful biracial baby girl I have ever seen. Her birth momma's story of giving her up to the Lord in prayer first and then giving her up for adoption is by far one of the most sacrificial gifts of obedience to God's call on her life at this time.

God is asking us to meditate and reflect on his Word day and night as he is watching over his world to see his Word performed. When we meditate on God and his Word, it honors him and gives us peace, assurance, and great hope.

Hope is found throughout the New and Old Testaments. We eagerly anticipate God's promises to be completely fulfilled in the second coming of the Messiah. The fact is that all creation waits in great expectation for him to be revealed again.

From the beginning of time until the day Christ returns, the whole of creation is groaning like childbearing. Yet there is hope as the Spirit and the bride say, "Come." The Holy Spirit intercedes for us with groans that our mind does not know. Our heart knows because it bears witness with him. When we think on the things of God, our position begins to shift into a heavenly point of view.

Ever since God cast Adam and Eve out of the garden due to their sin of disobedience toward God, we have been trying to get back to that place of being in the presence of the Lord. Peace was shattered the day Adam and Eve sinned against God, so as followers of Christ, we long for the restoration of shalom. We are longing for our true home, and that place is the very presence of God. The Spirit and the bride say, "Come."

Open the gates, and let the King of glory come in.

## Fighting Battles

*The LORD will fight for you; you need only to be still.*

—Exod. 14:14

Singing songs over and over can bring sweet peace, comfort, and truth into your heart and soul. As you memorize scripture and repeat passages in your mind, it becomes a tool to fight the enemy.

We fight our battles with praise to the Lord and prayers lifted up to God.

I often sing songs when there is a battle going on in my mind. The angel of the Lord encamps among those who fear him, so I call upon the angels to come and help me fight.

Almost every night, the enemy comes into my mind to start a fight with me. He brings up my sinful past, he tells me I'm not good enough or smart enough, and so on. He attacks my heart with thoughts of those near to me being hurt or harmed. I'm tired, weary, and worn down, so of course, Satan is going to lie to me. You'd think I would learn after all these years, but I tend to believe his lies. When I have had enough of the devil's deceit, I begin to fight back.

We can be strong in the might of the Lord when we put on the full armor of God. When we put on this armor, we can stand and fight against the schemes of the enemy.

You and I can stand our ground, fight, and then rest in the peace of God's truth, his Word.

Battles are being fought in the heavenly realms. Remember in the book of Job when the angels came to present themselves before the Lord, and Satan was there? (Job 1:6). In Daniel, chapter 10, we read how the angel was warring in the heavenly realms with Michael before he could give a message to Daniel.

I tend to start out of order in Ephesians 6:10–20 by putting on the helmet of salvation first. The battle is 99 percent in my mind, so I begin there to get some clarity. Recalling the moment I encountered and accepted the truth of God's love, I tell the enemy that I am the Lord's. I picture Christ's blood running down his head as he prayed in the garden. Jesus's head began hemorrhaging with sweats of blood as he wrestled with his Father to take that cup from him.

Next, I put on the breastplate of righteousness. I am his, and he is mine. God's Word tells me that I am redeemed, blessed, and forgiven. That is when I put on God's righteousness (Eph. 1). That makes me think about the breastplates the priests made in Exodus 28:10–30. They were embroidered with gold and set with 12 stones. These precious stones were ruby, topaz, garnet, emerald, sapphire, diamond, jacinth, agate, amethyst, berly, onyx, and jasper. Who wouldn't want to be adorned with these brilliant colors?

The belt of truth around my waist helps me hold it all together. Truth is absolute. You shall know the truth, and the truth shall set you free.

The gospel of peace is always ready to be proclaimed, first to yourself and then to others. Our feet help us stand firm when they are grounded in the Word of truth. How lovely are the feet of those who bring good news. We set our feet upon the rock, a firm foundation of our faith.

Whenever I am in a Bible study with younger women, they always make a statement that they would like to know scripture as I do. Lovingly, I share that studying God's Word inductively shaped my life, and praying who God is formed my heart. I'm older, and now that I look back on my life, nothing has been wasted. God's Word is buried within my heart, mind, soul, and spirit.

Now here's my favorite part: taking up the shield of faith. Before the Roman soldiers went into battle, they soaked their leather shields in the river. These shields (Greek: *hureos*) provided protection from head to toe. When the fiery darts were directed at the soldier, the water-soaked shield immediately extinguished the flames. The water of the Word washes over us and cleans us to be presented before our groom, spotless and pure.

We are to be alert, on guard, and ready to fight at all times. We are to pray at all times, in all occasions with all kinds of prayers. Boom! Call it a day, and go to sleep.

There are also power words to resist the devil and rebuke him, sending him away when he is trying to distract, devise, and destroy you. In Jesus's name, Satan must go away!

Read 2 Kings 3. The king of Israel set out with the king of Judah and the king of Edom to fight against the Moabites. King Mesha had rebelled against the king of Israel, and it was war time. For seven days, the kings and their armies marched through the desert of Edom and the south bend of the Dead Sea. They soon ran out of water and exclaimed that the Lord had called the three of them into battle together only to have them handed over to Moab. They needed water for their men and their animals.

They called on the prophet Elisha, a true prophet of the Lord. The pouring of water over his hands indicated his servanthood to God, and then he said, "Bring me a harpist."

When the music was playing, the Lord spoke through Elisha and informed the armies that they would have enough water, for it was an easy thing for God to do. The Lord came upon Elisha and spoke to him about the battle. He prophesied that they would win, and when they did win, they should cut down every good tree, stop up all the springs, and ruin every good field with stones.

Elisha told the kings to make ditches so they would fill up with water and the livestock could drink. When the Moabites heard that the kings had come to fight against every man, young and old, they stationed themselves at the border to fight. When the Moabites awoke the next morning as the sun was shining on the water, it looked red like blood. They thought the men had fought against themselves and slaughtered one another. The Israelites invaded the land and slaughtered the enemy.

The tragedy is that at the end of the fighting, the king of the Moabites realized that they were losing the battle, so he took his firstborn son and sacrificed him on the city wall. The Israelites were furious and withdrew. The enemy had purposely shed innocent blood. A divine judgment from God came upon the Israelites. It angered God that there had been a human sacrifice. Innocent bloodshed is forbidden in the Law (Lev. 18:21, 20:3).

We can fight our battles with authority when we plead the blood of Jesus over the situation. The blood is essential for our life, and it is precious to God, so costly that he gave innocent blood through his Son for all humanity to see his sacrifice for us all. Obedience and worship during a battle like the one in 2 Kings brings assurance that God fights our battles.

The battle belongs to the Lord (2 Chron. 20:15). Trust God. He is at work in your life. Due to the blood poured out on the cross, you can rest in God's sovereignty. If things are going well in your life or if you are in the battle of a lifetime, praising God is how you fight and thank him for all things. Remember, James tells us to "consider it pure joy . . . whenever you face trials of many kinds, because you know that the testing of your faith produces perseverance" (James 1:2–3).

When we meditate on God and his Word and then begin to pray, we can hear from him. We must be still; we must be silent as we listen. We can, indeed, pour the water of God's Word over our hearts and ask God to speak to us (Eph. 5:25–26).

*May these words of my mouth and this meditation of my heart*
*be pleasing in your sight,*
*LORD, my Rock and my Redeemer.*

—Ps. 19:14

There was a time when I ran anywhere from three to nine miles a day during the week with a wonderful group of friends. We would gather at the river to jog along the path, sharing about our lives and spurring one another on along the way. One everlasting memory was when I was on the trail by myself. It was cold, the trail was wet, and it was snowing. This was back in the '80s when we jogged without smartphones, MP3 players . . . or earbuds. As the snow was falling at a steady pace, it was peaceful and still, and the world seemed silent. I began to pray. It was a surreal moment, and I felt as if the Lord was right by my side in this one-person run. It became noticeably clear to me in that calm moment that I wanted to make this a practice of praying as I ran alone. I was meditating on the Lord while a peaceful setting surrounded me. I often go back to the tranquil run, and when war is after me, I stop and fight, knowing that the battle belongs to the Lord.

Now I walk in our neighborhood and at our small town's historical park and gardens to pray. The Lord leads me to intercede for the neighbors, our church staff, the state we live in, and our nation. Many days are filled with gratitude and a full heart for all God has given to me and done for me. Then there are times that I weep and lament over my sins and the state of affairs in the world. I often ask God to bless the people in their homes as I walk by. Ask the Lord for the opportunity to share the gospel with your community.

Prayer-walking is easy and satisfying as you put others before yourself to intercede on their behalf.

So lace up your running or walking shoes, and go out and enjoy the great outdoors as you stand in the gap for those around you. How lovely are the feet of those who bring good news.

## House Calls

> *Unless the LORD builds the house,*
> *the builders labor in vain.*
>
> —Ps. 127:1

Who ya gonna call? When there is serious spiritual warfare in your home, it is absolutely damaging to everyone in the house. It happens because sin is crouching at the door, ready to come in. It happens when there is unconfessed sin and you are off guard. It happens because Satan wants to rob, steal, and destroy. It happens.

Over the years, I've received phone calls in the middle of the night and made house calls for individuals who are experiencing tremendous stress due to an evil presence in their home. They often share that they even see the enemy in the corners of their room. They feel the evil, they see the enemy, they don't sleep, they can't eat, and the list goes on and on.

When I'm asked to come over to pray for someone, I begin praying the minute I get in my car to assist that person during this solemn event. With the Bible in one hand and anointing oil in the other, we begin the cleansing process outside the home first. We pray together and come boldly before the throne room, asking for Jesus's great authority to go before us. As we cross over the threshold, we stop and read Deuteronomy 6:4–10. I always suggest that the owners put scripture over every entrance in their home.

You can write the verses in small print and place them at the top of every door frame. If the person who is requesting the spiritual cleansing doesn't mind, you can anoint all the doorposts with oil.

There are many powerful scriptures to pray as you make the sign of the cross with the oil at each entrance. No, it's not magical, but it is scriptural. You can look up scriptures before you visit, and you can ask those requesting help to also have scriptures ready to pray over their home or apartment before you show up.

Always invite those who have asked you to come over to pray with you. Let them be part of the process. As you walk through each room of the home, stop and ask the Holy Spirit to speak to you and show you how to pray. Look around the room. What do you see? There are always clues to help you know how to pray for the home and the people who live there. Ask the Lord to show you and guide you in each and every room you go in. Ask for God to reveal in your spirit what is going on to cause these disturbances in the home and maybe in the individual. Don't feel rushed. Wait for the Lord to show you what to do next. The Holy Spirit will speak to your spirit.

Ask the Holy Spirit to give you scripture and insight every step of the way. The wonderful tool in the back of your Bible, the concordance, can help you find passages to pray. It is good to be silent at times and wait upon the Lord. He is there, and he desires for this home to be restored.

Once every room has been cleansed with scripture and prayer, go outside and in the garage, even praying over the attic. Call upon the warring angels to render service as Hebrews, chapter one, tells us they will. Ask if there is a family history of Masons, astrology, alcohol, or pornography. Trust me, those wanting to be set free will reveal the past. Shame is not to enter in. Always walk in love, forgiveness, and God's peace that surpasses all understanding in this situation. I've been to gravesites and walked through the streets of a small town in order for the past to be silenced. When healing comes and their soul is set free, it's peace at its finest.

I am no expert, and I highly recommend that you talk with your pastor or a biblical counselor to get help. In fact, this is a great place to share with you that I have not even touched on all the aspects of prayer, but you can have the joy of discovery once you dig deep into the Word.

All I know is that the Bible equips us for this work, and the Holy Spirit leads us in all truth. You shall know the truth and the truth will set you free. Pray without ceasing.

## Focus

> *Finally, brothers and sisters, whatever is true, whatever is noble, whatever is right, whatever is pure, whatever is lovely, whatever is admirable—if anything is excellent or praiseworthy—think about such things.*
>
> —Phil. 4:8

A few years ago, I attended a yearlong training program called the Institute. The purpose was to get to know God better and see how his story is my true story. With a biblical perspective, we studied Old and New Testament history and learned about the men and women who shaped our belief system. The study of God's Word is invigorating to my soul. This is God's theology at its best.

During the time of intense study, we wrote two doctoral papers and had several practicum assignments. As students of God's Word, we were challenged to go deeper into the heart of God and his Word and apply what we learned. On three different weekends, we had seminary professors come to teach, inspire, and challenge us in our faith. We wrote prayers and journaled our thoughts throughout the year of all that we were learning in the class. I was geeked out!

One evening, we were assigned to read a particular passage in Psalms to ourselves. After five minutes, our instructor, Kyle Worley, now pastor of Mosaic Church in Richardson, Texas, had a couple of people share what they had learned from scripture. Then he asked us to read it again for 10 more minutes and record any new findings from the passage. We then repeated the process one last time for 15 minutes, adding any new findings. Just like the wandering Israelites in the wilderness, many of us grumbled and thought, "How could we come up with any additional nuggets?" Our instructor had us read the short passage one last time. It became one of the most delightful exercises in the program. The Holy Spirit drew us nearer to himself by the written Word because we took time to submerge ourselves in that passage. Indeed, there was so much more to gain as we were seriously concentrating on the passage for a longer period of time than just simply reading it through only one time.

We ended up meditating on that passage for 30 minutes, and each passing moment revealed deeper truths to us.

Our instructor-pastor humbly shared how he spends several months in one passage, gleaning as much as the Holy Spirit wants to teach him regarding a certain passage in the Bible. This challenge is a good reminder for me to chew on God's Word and spend time with God to really get to know him and for him to conform me into the image of his Son.

## Still before the Lord

> Now then, stand still and see this great thing the LORD is about to do before your eyes!
>
> —1 Sam. 12:16

Here is an exercise designed to bring freedom and peace into your life when you are ready to sit in the presence of the Lord.

Grab a water bottle, open your Bible, have a journal by your side, turn everything off, sit down, and rest. Take a few minutes to relax. Maybe light a scented candle to enjoy the aroma and see the flame that flickers in your quiet room. Listen. Do you hear the heartbeat of your soul cry out for truth?

As you are alone and in the quietness of the moment, just breathe. Inhale, and now exhale, and ask God to forgive you of your sins. Ask God to bring these sins before you so you may confess them to him and be set free of those burdens you carry.

Rest, close your eyes, and envision his goodness toward you. Thank him for his loving-kindness, compassion, and grace throughout your life. On the cross, Jesus paid in full for your waywardness. He gave his life and very blood for the cleansing of your transgressions. You will begin to sense a freedom in every fiber of your being when you repent and confess the deepest and darkest sins to the Lord. Ask the Lord who you need to go to in order to confess your sins so you may be healed. If indeed you have wronged someone and sinned against them, you need to make it right with them. Whether you are in a leadership position or not, you are to walk in obedience and bring your offense into the light. This is a very hard thing to do, but I assure you from experience that it will set you free.

Inhale the air you breathe to sustain life. Begin to focus on the reality that God gave your life meaning and great purpose. As you take in air, envision taking the very essence of God's breath into your lungs. God the Creator made you in his image. He formed you, he loves you, and he knows you, but what is so astonishing is that he forgives you in all our failings. In fact, God says, "What sins?" Jesus paid the ultimate price for the sins of the world. As far as the east is from the west, God remembers your sins no more. I often grab my wooden, handheld cross from Israel and cling tightly to it as I pray. This handmade, olive tree wood cross brings about a calm, comforting vibe as I grasp what Jesus did on my behalf at Calvary. Enjoy his peace that surpasses all understanding through Christ Jesus.

Here are some practical ways to concentrate on a verse or a whole chapter in the Bible.

1. Write the scripture in a journal, on index cards, or on your computer device.
2. Place the scripture passages on your bathroom mirror and read them every time you look in the mirror.
3. Listen to the passage on your Bible app, and then hit repeat. Hit repeat again and again.
4. Read it in your TAG every day for months or even for an entire year.
5. Share your scripture findings with others.
6. Journal what you have learned by memorizing the passage.

## Entering into His Presence

> *You make known to me the path of life;*
> *you will fill me with joy in your presence,*
> *with eternal pleasures at your right hand.*

—Ps. 16:11

I'm a product of the '70s when music became one of the primary artistic expressions to pour out our hearts through the words of songs and hymns. Some of the lyrics we sang reflected what we were thinking and feeling during our adolescence. One of my favorite artists who I got to see perform several times wrote a powerful song about being in the presence of the Lord.

This rock star wrote and sang about having found the secret, and the way to live was finding peace in God.

As the musician was brought to his knees, he saw a blinding light and sensed God's presence. Like most performers back in the '70s, this singer was riddled with sex, drugs, and rock and roll. Experiencing God gave this brilliant guitarist a peace that the world just can't deliver. There is no better covering and protection than in God's light, peace, and love.

God set eternity in the hearts of all people, and when we enter into the company of a holy God, we are aware of his great love. All people of all nations will one day return to the Lord and worship him. God loves everyone, and he displays his love through people, creation, his Word, and his Spirit. God also allows all people to make the decision to love him or to follow the desires of their own fleshly heart. We all have a choice to make.

I have always enjoyed reading and studying the Old Testament. The book of Exodus is embedded with the tumultuous history of the Israelites and their quest to follow God.

Moses was called by God to lead the people out of Egypt's oppressive government and into the Promise Land, but God's chosen people struggled with the 40-year trek. Moses was spending purposeful time alone with God on Mount Sinai. The Lord was speaking to Moses about honoring the Sabbath and keeping it holy, and then God handed Moses two tablets of the testimony and made inscriptions with his finger on them.

The rebellious and corrupt action of the people caused God to burn with anger, and he wanted to destroy them due to their unruly sins. Moses sought the favor of the Lord on behalf of the people to save them from God's wrath against them. Moses heard and then began to see the people and their insubordinate activities as he came down the mountain. He, too, began to become angry and threw the tables down, breaking them into pieces.

Exodus 33 tells us that Moses had a tent some distance away from the camp. He called it the Tent of Meeting. The Lord would speak to Moses face-to-face as a friend. God told Moses to lead the people. Moses said, "Teach me your ways so I may know you and continue to find favor with you. Remember that this nation is your people" (Exod. 33:13). The Lord then spoke, "My Presence will go with you, and I will give you rest" (Exod. 33:14). Moses was bold and said to God, "Now show me your glory" (Exod. 33:18).

The Lord passed in front of Moses and proclaimed, "I will proclaim my name, the LORD, in your presence" (Exod. 33:19). There was mercy, compassion, kindness, and love so deep that it was likened to a father who loves his children deeply.

My prayer for you is to know this deep, compassionate love, that you would have an everlasting friendship with the King, and that His glory would surround you like a bright light as his radiance shines outward onto others so they too may come to know this merciful love. We were designed to be with the one who loves us so—our Creator-God.

It was time for the day to end. My brother and sister were up doing homework, and as the youngest, I was the first to bed. We had just come from our Wednesday night church service, and all I wanted to do was sing, not sleep. I was reflecting on the music from the evening service, enjoying feeling comfort and peace in the sanctuary. As the congregation was singing and came to the chorus in the song, a man began to worship in the most beautiful way. He whistled perfectly to the tune of the song as he worshiped the Lord with all his heart. At seven years old, I recall closing my eyes and thinking to myself that this must be what heaven will be like, people singing and worshiping in different languages.

As I was lying on my bed thinking about Jesus and not sleeping, my entire room lit up with a brilliant, blinding, bright, white light that engulfed the entire space. I knew it was Jesus. I felt his presence, and I was overtaken with great joy, peace, and love. I asked the Lord to come into my heart right then. He filled my heart, and apparently, we talked for a while. I don't remember the conversation but soon ran into my parents' room to tell them that I had asked Christ to be with me. They wondered who I was talking to as they heard me talking and singing with exhilaration.

Like my favorite guitarist, I too had experienced the presence of the Lord with a blinding, bright, white light. Our God is to be experienced.

Ezekiel received the prophetic call at the age of 30. Over and over again, we read that the Spirit of God lifted Ezekiel up, not only to encounter God but also to know and serve him. He made several remarks before the people to emphasize the priority of the Lord's character and his glory. For the sake of God's holy name, the people would know that God was the Lord and know the glory of the Lord. These statements were to encourage the exiles for future blessings to come. Ezekiel was speaking the truth that God is sovereign. He is in control over all things, and we must trust Him.

My point here is that if the Spirit of the living God was on these great patriarchs of the Old Testament and those of the new Way, then why aren't we engaging in the Spirit realm like they did? But wait! We can if we are asking the God of Abraham, Isaac, and Jacob—our God—to show us his glory. He will also allow us to experience His kindness and compassion with forgiveness, salvation, and freedom. He has given us his guaranteed deposit—the Holy Spirit. The Lord has allowed me to encounter him in the most phenomenal, supernatural ways.

The prayers of an understanding intercessor WILL create a meeting. And when the meeting comes to a close, something will have changed.[1]

## Communion

*While they were eating, Jesus took bread, and when he had given thanks, he broke it and gave it to his disciples, saying, "Take and eat; this is my body."*

*Then he took a cup, and when he had given thanks, he gave it to them, saying, "Drink from it, all of you. This is my blood of the covenant, which is poured out for many for the forgiveness of sins. I tell you, I will not drink from this fruit of the vine from now on until that day when I drink it new with you in my Father's kingdom."*

1. Dutch Sheets, *Intercessory Prayer* (Bloomington, MN: Bethany House Publishers, 1996), Google Books.

*When they had sung a hymn, they went out to the Mount of Olives.*

—Matt. 26:26–30

*They devoted themselves to the apostles' teaching and to fellowship, to the breaking of bread and to prayer. Everyone was filled with awe at the many wonders and signs performed by the apostles. All the believers were together and had everything in common. They sold property and possessions to give to anyone who had need. Every day they continued to meet together in the temple courts. They broke bread in their homes and ate together with glad and sincere hearts, praising God and enjoying the favor of all the people. And the Lord added to their number daily those who were being saved.*

—Acts 2:42–47

Communion is the most powerful and life-giving of the sacraments. It is how we remember what Christ did on the cross on our behalf. It is life and love. Christ's beautiful obedience is that it was with joy that he went to the cross.

Taking communion in the fellowship of believers is important for the health and life of the church. When we study Acts 2:42, we see the example of breaking bread together, praying, and having glad and sincere hearts as they were joined together. They took communion in the temple and in their homes, receiving their food and praising God.

The Greek word for fellowship is *koinonia*, expressing the ideal of being together for mutual benefit. The church body is to take time and create a space that renders an earnest time of reflection of the cross and all Christ went through. We should not rush this holy time of communion, and we should take this time to remember what his life was meant for here on earth. He came to set us free from the bonds of sin by sacrificing his body and his blood.

As you read scriptures about the crucifixion, you will be reading about how his body was torn, ripped apart, beaten, bruised, and bloody for your sins and mine. His entire body was wounded on our behalf. When you stop to think about the beatings Christ endured, you realize his wounds were from the top of his head to the soles of his feet, which were torched. From the crown of thorns on his head to the nails that fastened him to the tree, to the piercing sword that cut into his side, his body was broken for us.

Think about Jesus's pain and anguish, which began in the garden of Gethsemane. Can you even imagine the torment that took place in his mind and heart? This was the place where he brought his garden friends to be near him as he then went to be before God in isolation. It was indeed the Father, the Son, and the Holy Spirit kneeling at that rock to pray, and it was also the man called Jesus. He knew that obedience to his Father was the greatest gift to give—to die for the sins of all humanity—yet there was a supernatural struggle (1 Pet. 3:18).

One of the reasons this wrestling at the garden took place in Christ's mind was to help us understand that Jesus sympathizes with us in our time of need. When we struggle with the battle of the mind, we can remember how Christ prayed for himself and for the world.

Read Psalm 22.

Envision the blood shed for you. His body was covered with blood that was splattered, dripping, and flowing down onto the ground from the old, stained, wooden cross. Jesus was poured out as a drink offering for you.

Open your hands, and cup them together as if you were receiving water in them. Ask the Holy Spirit to fill you with the presence of the Lord. Think on him.

The walk to Emmaus is a beautiful road to travel. Our family had the privilege of participating in the 72-hour spiritual renewal weekend that was focused on taking the sacraments and listening to several talks about Christ's love. On the first evening of the event, we heard a talk about the cross, engaged in worship, and had the honor of taking communion to begin the retreat.

The women's weekend took place in a beautiful, old church with amazing architectural features. The sanctuary was darkened with only low lights and a huge wood cross that was center stage. The speaker asked us to write our sins down on the paper we had been given at the beginning of the evening. When we were ready to go down front, we were asked to lay our sins and burdens at the foot of the cross. Then our piece of paper would be nailed to the cross.

In that moment, I was sharply reminded of my life of folly and the countless sins set before me. I was frozen with grief and shame, yet I mustered up the courage to write my sins down and step into the aisle to lay my sins before the Lord. I stood in the walkway for a long time and then began to put one foot in front of the other. It was a long trek, yet the shame was already leaving my mind as I had asked God to forgive me in my seat. That was where the work began to take place—in my heart. The walk was in obedience to a holy God.

As I was placing my written words down at the base of the cross, I was reminded that this is where my husband is fond of saying, "We are all the same at the foot of the cross." Indeed, we are all the same at the foot of the cross. At that moment, God's love filled the very space where I was standing.

A woman from the leadership team handed me a piece of bread and spoke the words we have all heard so many times, yet that night it was more powerful and more real than ever before.

This is my body, broken on your behalf, which is for you; do this in remembrance of me. I placed the bread in my mouth and was completely overcome with the sense that I was consuming—eating—the body of Christ. I could barely swallow the bread as I placed it into my mouth. Revelation filled my mind as I realized in that moment that I was with Jesus on the cross. Certainly, my sins placed him on the cross, yet I knew in that moment what he did for us by his body being broken.

> *I have been crucified with Christ and I no longer live, but Christ lives in me. The life I now live in the body, I live by faith in the Son of God, who loved me and gave himself for me.*
>
> —Gal. 2:20

As the small cup of juice was given me to drink, my leader said, "This cup is the new covenant in my blood; do this, whenever you drink it, in remembrance of me" (1 Cor. 11:25).

A picture in my mind's eye came of Christ's beaten, bruised, and bloody beard partially ripped off his face. He had been spat upon, and the crown of thorns had been pressed deeply on his forehead, causing more blood to gush out of his head. I saw the risen Christ in my mind's eye and knew where he is today and that soon I would see him face-to-face for all eternity.

I drank the juice and wept. Soon, my heart began to rejoice as I was profoundly aware that my name is written in the Lamb's Book of Life and that soon I will have a new name given to me by God and that name will be inscribed on a white stone (Rev. 2:17). I knew all of this beforehand, but once again, I had an experience with the living God in the dimly lit haven.

I longed for the day when we all will worship him together and break bread with one another in his presence. When we lift up our glass of wine in honor of God, we will see him more clearly. Oh, what fellowship with my Lord! We will have that new name written on a white stone. That name will be chosen by the Lord and will reveal his affections for us. Your very essence, your character, and your nature define who you are. The meaning of our name represents the gospel. Find out the biblical meaning of your name, and find comfort that God has blessed you with an important name. I also want to encourage you to have a life scripture that you memorize. That will be a passage that you seem to always run to throughout your life.

Let me show you something I have recently learned. Read Genesis, chapter five, and write down the name of the 10 men from this chapter—Adam, Seth, Enosh, Kenan, Mahalalel, Jared, Enoch, Methuselah, Lamech, and Noah.

Google each of the Hebrew names, and write down their meanings next to each name.

Man, appointed or anointed, moral sorrow, blessing, praise of God, come down, dedicated, hid death, shall send, and rest.

People are appointed unto moral sorrow. The blessed God of praise shall come down, dedicated to his death, and shall send strong rest and comfort.

Do the same for the 12 tribes of Israel found in the book of Deuteronomy.

Behold the son who is obedient. Joining in praise is the dwelling place of honor. There is great reward, for God is my judge. There is fortune, happiness, and blessings even in my struggles and strife. May Jehovah give great increase.

Acts 17:26–28 is such a comforting passage to me. From one man, God made every nation that the people should inhabit the whole earth, and he determines the times set for them and the exact places where they should live. God did this so people would seek him and perhaps reach out to him and find him, though he is not far from each of us. For in him we live and move and have our being. As some poets have said, we are his offspring. Looking a

Boggs Lake, Frisco, Colorado

little further in the passage, you will read that God commands all people everywhere to repent. Remember that.

In Revelation 19:11–13, we also learn that Jesus will have a new name that has never been defiled, for he is King of kings and Lord of lords.

## Buckle Up! Here We Go. Better Yet, Unbuckle!

*Prayer Talk*

> *My mouth will speak words of wisdom;*
> *the meditation of my heart will give you understanding.*
> *—Ps. 49:3*

> *However, as it is written:*
> *"What no eye has seen, what no ear has heard,*
> *and what no human mind has conceived"—*
> *the things God has prepared for those who love him—*
> *these are the things God has revealed to us by his Spirit.*

*The Spirit searches all things, even the deep things of God. For who knows a person's thoughts except their own spirit within them? In the same way no one knows the thoughts of God except the Spirit of God. What we have received is not the spirit of the world, but the Spirit who is from God, so that we may understand what God has freely given us. This is what we speak, not in words taught us by human wisdom but in words taught by the Spirit, explaining spiritual realities with Spirit-taught words. The person without the Spirit does not accept the things that come from the Spirit of God but considers them foolishness, and cannot understand them because they are discerned only through the Spirit. The person with the Spirit makes judgments about all things, but such a person is not subject to merely human judgments, for,*

*"Who has known the mind of the Lord so as to instruct him?"*

*But we have the mind of Christ.*

—1 Cor. 2:9–16

*And pray in the Spirit on all occasions with all kinds of prayers and requests. With this in mind, be alert and always keep on praying for all the Lord's people.*

—Ephesians 6:18

*But you, dear friends, by building yourselves up in your most holy faith and praying in the Holy Spirit.*

—Jude 20

*But the Advocate, the Holy Spirit, whom the Father will send in my name, will teach you all things and will remind you of everything I have said to you.*

—John 14:26

One of the reasons the Holy Spirit was given to us is to have discernment poured out to us when we ask for it. First Corinthians, chapters 12, 13, and 14, are packed with the all-sufficient scriptures on the subject of praying in the Spirit (tongues). Personally, I wrestled with the concept of tongues for a long time until I experienced the Holy Spirit in a new and fresh way.

I've been in the church all my life, and the one thing that has rarely been talked about, much less preached about, is the subject of the Holy Spirit. In many ways, that's why I believe the Lord told me it was time to write a book on prayer, to speak up and to testify of the workings of the Holy Spirit. For years, my close friend Rachael has been prompting me to write a book on prayer. I would start writing, but nothing would take hold. I'm a poor speller and dyslexic, and there is no way I could ever put my thoughts down on paper. There is no way the Lord would have someone like me write a book.

After an evening of the A.C.T.S. way of prayer with some new friends, one young woman, Molly, asked for my phone number, asking me to adopt her. I enjoy mentoring, so I naturally gave her my number. Several days passed, and I received a text from Molly. She shared that as I was leading the group on how to pray the four steps of prayer, during the time of praising God for who he is, she was healed. The very moment I read her words, the Holy Spirit spoke to my heart—"It's time." I knew exactly what the Lord meant. I began writing and could not stop for several months.

I heard the instruction to write on prayer, so I did. A year passed. I kept waiting for the Lord to give my next instructions. He simply had asked me to write it, so I did. Attending a Bible study on the book of Ephesians and taking notes as the teacher was speaking, I heard the speaker use the word *publish* in one of her sentences. God whispered, "Jana, that was for you."

God is always speaking. Sometimes, I listen.

The Trinity is a beautiful display of God's great artistic gift of himself to us in three beautiful expressions. We read and see that God is sovereign over all things and that he is the one true Godhead over all peoples everywhere. Jesus, the Son of God, became incarnate in order for us to see God in the flesh. Jesus would lay down his life, taking the sins of the world on his body and being crucified by you and me for our many sins. He died, was buried, and rose on the third day. Jesus proved the Bible to be authentic. Hallelujah! Jesus was truly resurrected. The Holy Spirit remains a mystery to many in the church. The church wants to be safe and not get "too crazy" experiencing God, Jesus, and the power of the Holy Spirit.

I find it most interesting that Jesus himself when baptized in the Jordan River by the Holy Spirit was filled with the presence of the Holy Spirit in order to do ministry on behalf of his Father. If Jesus received this indwelling and filling of the Spirit, I need to also be filled with that same dynamite. We follow the example of water baptism, but what about the baptism of fire and the Spirit?

Now remember, I was raised in a Baptist church, and I am still serving in that same denomination today. For more than 20 years, my husband and I served in a conservative Methodist church, and that is where I experienced the reality of the Holy Spirit alongside thousands of teenagers from summer camps.

Maybe it's time for the church to study, teach, train, and equip the saints to know more about the Holy Spirit in order to walk in a bold power while sharing the gospel of truth. If we daily need to take up his cross and follow him, then we must also need to be filled with the very nature of the Trinity so we can love others with this amazing grace.

I know that the church at large has concerns about the function of the Holy Spirit because the church has often misused this beautiful gift. We were in Tulsa when there was an outpouring of the Holy Spirit in the '80s, and we saw and experienced his power unleashed. We experienced the good use and the misuse of the work of the Holy Ghost.

Now that we live in Texas, we hear stories of that same kind of outpouring that happened all over Texas and in other states as well. The sad part is that some of those experiences were not 100 percent legit. So the caution is honorable to want to weigh out "events" of the Spirit, but I also want to encourage the church to not quench the Spirit. When you walk in integrity and serve, then the leadership of your local gathering of the saints will more than likely be engaged with you in a conversation about his power.

## God Created Man in His Image and Then Breathed the Breath of Life into Him

> *Then the* LORD *God formed a man from the dust of the ground and breathed into his nostrils the breath of life, and the man became a living being.*
>
> —Gen. 2:7

We see this life-breathing action again in John 20:22. This takes place after the resurrection of Christ and when he was speaking to the disciples.

> *On the evening of that first day of the week, when the disciples were together, with the doors locked for fear of the Jewish leaders, Jesus came and stood among them and said, "Peace be with you!" After he said this, he showed them his hands and side. The disciples were overjoyed when they saw the Lord.*
>
> *Again, Jesus said, "Peace be with you! As the Father has sent me, I am sending you." And with that he breathed on them and said, "Receive the Holy Spirit."*
>
> —John 20:19–22

All four Gospels refer to Jesus as the baptizer of the Holy Spirit (Matt. 3:11, Mark 1:8, Luke 3:16, John 1:33–34).

## The Baptism of the Holy Spirit Is a Gift

> *If you then, though you are evil, know how to give good gifts to your children, how much more will your Father in heaven give the Holy Spirit to those who ask Him!*
>
> —Luke 11:13

> *Peter replied, "Repent and be baptized, every one of you, in the name of Jesus Christ for the forgiveness of your sins. And you will receive the gift of the Holy Spirit."*
>
> —Acts 2:38

*I am going to send you what my Father has promised: but stay in the city until you have been clothed with power from on high.*

—Luke 24:49

*On one occasion, while he was eating with them, he gave them this command: "Do not leave Jerusalem, but wait for the gift my Father promised, which you have heard me speak about. For John baptized with water, but in a few days you will be baptized with the Holy Spirit."*

—Acts 1:4–5

This gift of the Holy Spirit was to empower the saints to be bold and share the good news of eternal life through Christ (Acts 1:8, 2:4; Mark 16:17; 1 Cor. 14:15, 18).

*But you will receive power when the Holy Spirit comes on you; and you will be my witnesses in Jerusalem, and in all Judea and Samaria, and to the ends of the earth.*

—Acts 1:8

## Since the Beginning, the Holy Spirit Was There

*Now the earth was formless and empty, darkness was over the surface of the deep, and the Spirit of God was hovering over the waters.*

—Gen. 1:2

## Jesus Received the Holy Spirit

*When all the people were being baptized, Jesus was baptized too. And as He was praying, heaven was opened and the Holy Spirit descended on Him in bodily form like a dove. And a voice came from heaven: "You are my Son, whom I love; with you I am well pleased."*

—Luke 3:21–22

After Christ's baptism, he was led by the Spirit to return to Jordan, and he went into the desert to be tempted by Satan. Yet every time he spoke scripture to answer the evil one, Jesus had the power of the Holy Spirit to withstand the enemy's schemes.

## We Are Made in His Image

*Then God said, "Let us make mankind in our image, in our likeness, so that they may rule over the fish in the sea and the birds in the sky, over the livestock and all the wild animals, and over all the creatures that move along the ground."*

—Genesis 1:26

## We Can Have the Mind of Christ

*"Who has known the mind of the Lord so as to instruct him?" But we have the mind of Christ.*

—1 Cor. 2:16

*Then he called the crowd to him along with his disciples and said: "Whoever wants to be my disciple must deny themselves and take up their cross and follow me."*

—Mark 8:34

*In their hearts humans plan their course,*
*    but the LORD establishes their steps.*

—Prov. 16:9

*He has made everything beautiful in its time. He has also set eternity in the human heart; yet no one can fathom what God has done from beginning to end.*

—Eccles. 3:11

## We Can Be Filled with the Spirit

*The Spirit himself testifies with our spirit that we are God's children.*
—Rom. 8:16

*I speak the truth in Christ—I am not lying, my conscience confirms it through the Holy Spirit.*
—Rom. 9:1

*As for you, the anointing you received from him remains in you, and you do not need anyone to teach you. But as his anointing teaches you about all things and as that anointing is real, not counterfeit—just as it has taught you, remain in him.*
—1 John 2:27

## God Speaks to People through His Word

*All Scripture is God-breathed and is useful for teaching, rebuking, correcting and training in righteousness.*
—2 Tim. 3:16

## God Speaks to Us through His Son, Jesus

*The Spirit himself testifies with our spirit that we are God's children.*
—Rom. 8:16

*Jesus said to her, "I am the resurrection and the life. The one who believes in me will live, even though they die; and whoever lives by believing in me will never die. Do you believe this?"*
—John 11:25–26

*Jesus answered, "I am the way and the truth and the life. No one comes to the Father except through me."*
—John 14:6

*I am the good shepherd; I know my sheep and my sheep know me.*

—John 10:14

## God Speaks to Us through Nature

*For since the creation of the world God's invisible qualities— his eternal power and divine nature—have been clearly seen, being understood from what has been made, so that people are without excuse.*

—Rom. 1:20

## God Speaks through Other Believers

*But the wisdom that comes from heaven is first of all pure; then peace-loving, considerate, submissive, full of mercy and good fruit, impartial and sincere. Peacemakers who sow in peace reap a harvest of righteousness.*

—James 3:17–18

*But encourage one another daily, as long as it is called "Today," so that none of you may be hardened by sin's deceitfulness.*

—Heb. 3:13

## God Speaks through Music

*After consulting the people, Jehoshaphat appointed men to sing to the LORD and to praise him for the splendor of his holiness as they went out at the head of the army, saying:*

*"Give thanks to the LORD,*
   *for his love endures forever."*

—2 Chron. 20:21

## God Speaks through Circumstances

*And we know that in all things God works for the good of those who love him, who have been called according to his purpose. For those God foreknew he also predestined to be conformed to the image of his Son, that he might be the firstborn among many brothers and sisters.*

—Rom. 8:28–29

## God Speaks through His Spirit

*And I will ask the Father, and he will give you another advocate to help you and be with you forever—the Spirit of truth. The world cannot accept him, because it neither sees him nor knows him. But you know him, for he lives with you and will be in you.*

—John 14:16–17

*Don't you know that you yourselves are God's temple and that God's Spirit dwells in your midst?*

—1 Cor. 3:16

## God Speaks through Prayer

*In the same way, the Spirit helps us in our weakness. We do not know what we ought to pray for, but the Spirit himself intercedes for us through wordless groans. And he who searches our hearts knows the mind of the Spirit, because the Spirit intercedes for God's people in accordance with the will of God.*

—Rom. 8:26–27

## God Is Spirit—People Commune with God through His Spirit

*God is spirit, and his worshipers must worship in the Spirit and in truth.*

—John 4:24

*But because of his great love for us, God, who is rich in mercy, made us alive with Christ even when we were dead in transgressions—it is by grace you have been saved.*

—Eph 2:4–5

## How Many Baptisms Are There? Water – Fire – Spirit

*Make every effort to keep the unity of the Spirit through the bond of peace. There is one body and one Spirit, just as you were called to one hope when you were called; one Lord, one faith, one baptism; one God and Father of all, who is over all and through all and in all.*

—Eph. 4:3–6

*"I baptize you with water for repentance. But after me comes one who is more powerful than I, whose sandals I am not worthy to carry. He will baptize you with the Holy Spirit and fire."*

—Matt. 3:11

*On one occasion, while he was eating with them, he gave them this command: "Do not leave Jerusalem, but wait for the gift my Father promised, which you have heard me speak about. For John baptized with water, but in a few days, you will be baptized with the Holy Spirit."*

—Acts 1:4–5

*I baptize you with water, but he will baptize you with the Holy Spirit.*

—Mark 1:8

*And I myself did not know him, but the one who sent me to baptize with water told me, "The man on whom you see the Spirit come down and remain is the one who will baptize with the Holy Spirit."*

—John 1:33

*John answered them all, "I baptize you with water. But one who is more powerful than I will come, the straps of whose sandals I am not worthy to untie. He will baptize you with the Holy Spirit and fire."*

—Luke 3:16

*"If you love me, keep my commands. And I will ask the Father, and he will give you another advocate to help you and be with you forever—the Spirit of truth. The world cannot accept him, because it neither sees him nor knows him. But you know him, for he lives with you and will be in you."*

—John 14:15–17

*But now I am going to him who sent me. None of you asks me, "Where are you going?" Rather, you are filled with grief because I have said these things. But very truly I tell you, it is for your good that I am going away. Unless I go away, the Advocate will not come to you; but if I go, I will send him to you. When he comes, he will prove the world to be in the wrong about sin and righteousness and judgment: about sin, because people do not believe in me; about righteousness, because I am going to the Father, where you can see me no longer; and about judgment, because the prince of this world now stands condemned.*

*I have much more to say to you, more than you can now bear. But when he, the Spirit of truth, comes, he will guide you into all the truth. He will not speak on his own; he will speak only what he hears, and he will tell you what is yet to come. He will glorify me because it is from me that he will receive what he will make known to you. All that belongs to the Father is mine. That is why I said the Spirit will receive from me what he will make known to you.*

—John 16:5–15

## When Did the Holy Spirit Fill the Disciples?

After Jesus's death, burial, and resurrection, Jesus was showing the disciples his hands and side, and then he breathed on them, and they were filled with the Holy Spirit. That was before Pentecost.

> *On the evening of that first day of the week, when the disciples were together, with the doors locked for fear of the Jewish leaders, Jesus came and stood among them and said, "Peace be with you!" After he said this, he showed them his hands and side. The disciples were overjoyed when they saw the Lord.*
>
> *Again Jesus said, "Peace be with you! As the Father has sent me, I am sending you." And with that he breathed on them and said, "Receive the Holy Spirit."*
>
> —John 20:19–22

## What Did Jesus Instruct His Disciples to Do after They Had the Holy Spirit in Them?

> *I am going to send you what my Father has promised; but stay in the city until you have been clothed with power from on high.*
>
> —Luke 24:49

> *But you will receive power when the Holy Spirit comes on you; and you will be my witnesses in Jerusalem, and in all Judea and Samaria, and to the ends of the earth.*
>
> —Acts 1: 8

## Did Jesus Experience Holy Spirit Baptism?

> *At that time Jesus came from Nazareth in Galilee and was baptized by John in the Jordan. Just as Jesus was coming up out of the water, he saw heaven being torn open and the Spirit descending on him like a dove. And a voice came from heaven: "You are my Son, whom I love; with you I am well pleased."*
>
> —Mark 1:9–11

*When all the people were being baptized, Jesus was baptized too. And as he was praying, heaven was opened and the Holy Spirit descended on him in bodily form like a dove. And a voice came from heaven: "You are my Son, whom I love; with you I am well pleased."*

—Luke 3:21–22

*In the last days, God says,*
  *I will pour out my Spirit on all people.*
*Your sons and daughters will prophesy,*
  *your young men will see visions,*
  *your old men will dream dreams.*

—Acts 2:17

How do we experience the Holy Spirit baptism? Ask.

*Ask and it will be given to you; seek and you will find; knock and the door will be opened to you. For everyone who asks receives; the one who seeks finds; and to the one who knocks, the door will be opened.*

—Matt. 7:7–8

Receive the Holy Spirit. Accept the Holy Spirit. Ask for the Holy Spirit. Drink in the filling of the Holy Spirit. Now, yield to the power of the Holy Spirit. Ready. Set. Go.

We want to give God control over our lives. God has a gift for us like a gentle dove, the indwelling of the Holy Spirit. We certainly receive this gift at the very moment we ask Jesus to be Lord of our lives.

*And you also were included in Christ when you heard the message of truth, the gospel of your salvation. When you believed, you were marked in him with a seal, the promised Holy Spirit, who is a deposit guaranteeing our inheritance until the redemption of those who are God's possession—to the praise of his glory.*

—Eph. 1:13–14

God wants to commune with you and me on a spiritual level. Intellect is a wonderful gift from the Lord; in fact, it is what makes great theologians. To know God's Word and make him known is our highest calling. However, it is much more freeing to let go and let our spirit talk to God. To pray to God and worship him in a way that is very foreign to us is how God has allowed us to communicate with him.

If you were driving a self-park car and it was time to parallel park, the first thing the car would tell you to do is to let go of the steering wheel. The next act of surrendering to your car's command is to take your foot off the brake.

God wants us to let go of our control over our hearts and lives and ask him to take control. We also must not hit the brake and decide when not to let him drive.

We are spirit beings and must worship God in Spirit and in truth:
Genesis 1:26
Thessalonians 5:23
John 4:24
Job 32

## Story One

Both sides of our family had gathered for a fun barbeque at our home one year in mid-July. The kids were in the backyard playing catch with their uncle, and "Martha" here (that would be me) was cleaning up from dinner. Our son, Daniel, came bolting through the back door shaking, crying, and proclaiming he had just hurt his sister very badly. Daniel was in elementary school, and our daughter was in the first grade. Uncle Jimmy had been pitching softballs to our son, and a couple of balls had fallen to the ground. Daniel had an old wooden bat in his hands, and just at the time he was swinging at a thrown ball, Haven came up right behind him, ready to pick up the softball that had dropped to the ground. Daniel accidentally hit Haven in the forehead with a lot of force with the bat. Blood was everywhere—on the ground, on her shirt, and all over the patio. My mom was with Daniel, assuring him that everything was going to be okay; my husband was calling the hospital; and I had scooped our daughter into my arms and carried her over to a chair to sit down as

I began applying pressure to her forehead. It was just Haven and I in the yard, so I thought, but little did I know that the Holy Spirit was with us in that moment.

I was incredibly calm, which, by the way, is totally not like me in a situation like this. Holding the palm of my hand on her head, I began thanking Jesus. I kept saying, "Thank you, Jesus. Thank you, Jesus." And out of my innermost being came a language I didn't know. I stopped for a moment, looked at my sweet little girl, and felt an amazing presence of peace over us. I began praying those unfamiliar words over and over again.

*My mouth will speak words of wisdom;*
*the meditation of my heart will give you understanding.*
—Ps. 49:3

Family began coming outside, and I knew it was time to go to the hospital. Our neighbors were outside in their front yards as we were loading up, and we asked them to pray for us as we headed out.

You know how emergency rooms can be filled with panic in the air? It can get really loud as you hear people making decisions on care and hear crying from people in great pain. In our makeshift curtained room, our neighbors who have eight children came to the hospital to pray with us. As we bowed our heads and trusted the Lord's work to be done for our daughter, there was an overwhelming calm that engulfed our small space as we waited for Haven to be cared for by the doctor and nurse. Our prayers went out of the room like smoke billowing from the floor flowing down the hallway. Within minutes the entire emergency room was silent and calm. The Holy Spirit was evident as he moved among the people. Prayer calms us, even in the most stressful moments.

We sat there with the doctor as he put stitches in our daughter's forehead. He noticed the words on Haven's blood-stained T-shirt—Peter Rock—a vacation Bible school shirt.

The doctor was excited since his wife was in a Precept Bible study at our church. I taught Precept there. He asked what Haven's favorite song was, and he sang it to her as he sewed her up. I was weeping and had to look away as he worked on her forehead. The presence of the Lord was in that room and in the hallways of that hospital. The next day, we met with our neighbors and dear friends who are charismatic pastors. Mark and I had questions about my experience of praying in tongues and what happened in the emergency room. We prayed. Mark shared that he had never before felt such love all throughout his body, mind, and heart.

I asked our trusted friends and pastors about praying in tongues. These godly friends gave me the best advice, "Seek the giver of the gift, not the gift." The gift will always point to Jesus.

I began the quest of seeking God for the rest of that summer with every fiber of my being. Still today, I desire to study the Word of God, pray, and simply want to know Christ in a deeper and more intimate way than the day before. I desire to experience him.

More than 25 years have passed since my first time praying in my spirit in an unknown language. To be completely honest, I am just now learning to use my prayer language daily. As I connect with God on a deeper level, I am learning to fight battles in my spirit, too. When I pray in the spirit, I am talking to God's Holy Spirit. My usual words will fail, but the prayer language does not.

As I look back through my entire life, I can say with confidence that my life has been defined by the powerful working of the Holy Spirit. I have often joked about how God loves the simple minded and has had to hit me over the head with a bolt of lightning in order for me to see God more clearly. He has opened my heart and eyes of understanding over the years to see him, and I am now grateful for my simple ways.

## Story Two

I was born with a deformed and twisted leg. My mom tells me that at 18 months, while in a specialist's office as she sat down to pray, my leg miraculously straightened out. My mom simply stated that I was the Lord's and that she would raise me to love him. The Lord healed my crooked leg that day. Then God healed my bent-out-of-shape stony heart and made it a heart of malleable flesh. That was the day I received Christ. Still today, God walks with me and makes my crooked path straight. To God is the glory.

## Story Three

I was attending a Bible study with a friend, and at the close of the study, the teacher asked if I needed prayer. I said no thank you. He then asked if I was Holy Spirit filled. I shared this truth: "I received the Holy Spirit when I accepted Christ," which, by the way, is 100 percent true. The pastor prayed over me to receive the filling of the Spirit and to have evidence with a gifting. He also had a word for me that I believe has come to fruition in my life. I went home and prayed all through the night, asking for this gift of the Holy Spirit.

Early the next morning, I turned over in my bed and saw in my mind's eye an angel kneeling with outstretched hands, praying over me. I felt an anointing power over my life in that instant. Maybe this blessing was sent from God through my guardian angel. I saw a beautiful, white being, and just as I beheld him, he vanished (Heb. 1:14, Ps. 34:7).

## Story Four

A group of my friends and I were sitting on the floor of my parents' study to pray before the group left to drive back to Florida from Oklahoma. During the prayer, in my mind's eye and in my friends' as well, we all saw Jesus's robe. His hands were holding our hands as we prayed. He was lifting us up off the ground. We all felt such a peace come over us in that moment. We were all single at the time, and having Christ's presence become a real experience brought an assurance that we all are truly in the palm of God's hands. Sounds crazy, but it really happened, and I have hesitated to share these stories for fear of what people might think.

Studying about tongues in scripture has led me to the conclusion that you can ask for it. It is simply talking to God through the Holy Spirit that resides within you.

> But you, dear friends, by building yourselves up in your most holy faith and praying in the Holy Spirit.
>
> —Jude 20

Romans chapter eight has been called "Life through the Spirit." Here are a few verses that inform us about the Holy Ghost. These words speak truth on earth and in people's spirits. "The Spirit himself testifies with our spirit that we are God's children" (Rom. 8:16). The whole of creation is groaning, awaiting Christ's return. The rocks will cry out, and the trees will clap their hands as we wait for the Lord. We also read that the Spirit groans inwardly:

> *In the same way, the Spirit helps us in our weakness. We do not know what we ought to pray for, but the Spirit himself intercedes for us through wordless groans. And he who searches our hearts knows the mind of the Spirit, because the Spirit intercedes for God's people in accordance with the will of God.*
> —Rom. 8:26–27

Praying the names, attributes, and character of God made me grow into a stronger personal and cherished relationship with God. Teaching Precept Bible studies and serving in both children's and youth ministries trained me up as a young adult.

Praying in the spirit edifies and builds you up in your innermost being. The most freeing truth for me about praying this way is that when I pray in this tongue (that I don't understand), I understand that it is my spirit communing with God. It's liberating to know that my pure heart is speaking to my Maker. Because let's face it, I am not pure in heart.

## Story Five

Late one afternoon while I was jogging, listening to music through my ear buds and singing out loud, I had an overwhelming experience of joy and revelation knowledge. I stopped the music and began singing in my spirit. Joy and peace infiltrated my entire body with chills as tears flowed down my face. Suddenly, I knew in my spirit that when we arrive in heaven and stand side-by-side with our brothers and sisters from all over the world, we will be united with our voices singing the same song together. There is a song we have deep inside us that will unite all nations in one accord as we sing for God's glory.

## Story Six

I was really sad and deeply depressed. I was greatly missing my godly mom who had taught me so much about the Lord. Mark and I had just moved to Texas after ministering in our local church in Tulsa for more than 24 years with family and friends. We were known in the community and also served outside the church. I was missing our kids and our hometown community. I had a lot of bottled up hurt in my heart; in fact, I was mad at God.

One evening while I was in bed, tears flowing down my cheeks, I was really mourning the loss of my mom. Out of my innermost being came an utterance, a moaning from the pit of my stomach. I remember thinking that this is what Romans 8 is talking about because I didn't know how to pray in my depression.

The Lord took over and prayed on behalf of my troubled heart. My spirit bore witness with his. In this time of God's grace, my depression only lasted around two years. There were several times I wanted to just end my life, and hope was not to be found in my natural way of thinking. I have a supportive, loving husband, great kids, and wonderful friends, yet this blanket would not lift off my heart and soul. I was reading scripture, going to church, and serving in ministry, but I still had a heavy burden of missing my mom, family, friends, and home.

When I began praying daily for the staff at our church, the depression lifted. I then began walking in jubilation for several weeks. I am grateful to the Lord for entrusting me with the gift of a crushed heart, which helped me understand, sympathize, and care when others are walking that road of heaviness. My journey of depression led me to become a certified biblical counselor so I could share the truth of God's Word in the midst of others' pain and sorrow.

There is always hope, and God's timing is always perfect. My life has been marked with a pull to understand and know the Holy Spirit as well as loving on and helping the wounded. Most churches have faltered in not teaching in depth about the subject of the Holy Ghost, and I believe there has been a grave misunderstanding of God's power, love, and teaching of grace.

## Story Seven

My husband and I were asked to work in the student ministry at our church in Tulsa. Dick Read had been observing us for a while and apparently came to the conclusion that we were just crazy enough to volunteer to serve in the church's youth ministry. We fell in love with teenagers and continued in that ministry for 18 years. Teaching Bible study, leading small groups every week, nights of worship in our home, prayer nights, Breakaway worship time once a month, fall and summer camps, mission trips, and local ministry became some of the best years of our lives.

At one of our fall retreats, I led a small group of girls who were all cheerleaders or on the pom squad. Discussion time was over, and I asked if someone would like to close in prayer. To this day, I smile as I remember one of the girls saying, "Ready? Okay!" All the girls clasped their hands together with a clap and nodded their heads. We laughed our way through that prayer. Prayer can be fun.

Dayspring. Need I say more? Those who walked through those muggy, hot, sticky summer days and nights for a week in Tahlequah, Oklahoma, know that the word *Dayspring* alone brings back the memories of the Holy Spirit encounters at camp for several years.

What everyone encountered—usually by the third day of camp year after year—was spectacular. They were Holy Spirit meetings with God.

It must have been 100 degrees toward the end of the day, and a storm was brewing. The speaker, Keith Wheeler, who has carried the cross around the world, was our speaker that summer.

All the leaders and the worship team had been in prayer throughout the day, and we were eagerly waiting for what the Lord had in store for us that evening.

The 300-plus high school students gathered in the open-air tabernacle to worship the Lord with abandonment. There was such liberty in the Lord at Dayspring camps, and I really miss those spirit-filled evenings in worship.

The kids were so excited to hear about Keith's adventures all over the world carrying his 82-pound wooden cross and sharing the gospel of Jesus to a lost world.

I had stepped out of the tabernacle to look out on the Barren Fork River to pray and do just a bit of dancing with some of the other free-at-heart teenagers. I had turned my back on the gathering to pray when a huge clap of thunder and bolt of lightning knocked out all the lights in the entire campground. It was pitch black, and my first thought was, "Oh no! I'm blind. But wait! You have done that before, God."

The generator kicked on. When I turned around, I saw all 300 students on their faces before the God of creation.

I looked over at Keith who had the microphone in his hand. Eyes wide open and pointing at the mic, we both were amazed at the power of the Lord that night. At the end of the evening while the band was playing, it began to rain softly with rolls of thunder and lightning continuing in the background.

The band began to transition into playing acoustically, and the students began to sing with great fervor and passion. Then, the band simply set their instruments down and walked off the stage, and the campers sang a capella for the rest of the evening. The rolls of thunder and the lightning dancing in the darkened clouds above were accompanied by the sound of singing angels joining in with us—or was it the other way around?

There were healings, restored hearts, salvation, and freedom at Dayspring year after year after year. One teenager who could barely walk through the campgrounds due to a heart condition was healed of his heart disease. That evening, he began running throughout the camp shouting accolades unto the Lord.

We had students receive powerful joy as continuous laughter broke out among them. We had to move them to another smaller, open-air building not too far away. Many of these students had hard family dynamics and had to deal with abusive and very difficult situations in their homes. This summer camp was a reprieve from the abuse. There were young people who in an instant looked like they were drunk with bloodshot eyes and a frozen stance. They were filled with the presence of the Lord, and what came with that indwelling was incredible peace.

One student was transported (in his spirit) into the heavenlies and was flying over the nations. What an incredible thing to experience! All these happenings were to build up the body of Christ to go and tell the world what the Lord had done in them at camp and ultimately for the glory of the Lord. God revealed himself in the most powerful ways at that little Oklahoma camp.

There was also a large group of these students who went to serve on the mission field, both short-term and full-time missions in various countries. The Lord called many of them to go to the nations, and they responded, "Yes, Lord."

## Original Marks

My husband is very creative, and his mind is always coming up with innovative ideals. He likes to connect people and watch how they in turn help one another. I want to share with you some of the resourceful tools we came up with to lead a small group, home group, community group, and so on.

One cold, wintry Sunday morning in the 1980s, we loaded up our big, black suburban with senior high school students and headed to the local cemetery. As we walked through the quiet grounds with the bare trees, crisp air, and solemn atmosphere, we focused on the beauty and peacefulness that engulfed us. After observing hundreds of headstones and thinking about our own mortality, we headed back to the warmth of our cars. Respectfully and with reverence, we shared what we felt as we strolled through the park filled with the past of people's lives on markers in stone. Mark pointed out the date when a person was born and the date of their death. He shared how the very short dash between those dates represented the person's life. He proposed a question: "What will your dash look like to others when you are gone?" What does your dash look like today? How are you living for the one who gave you life? Will your time on earth represent God or self? And when you stand before God one day to be accountable for your life, will you have fulfilled your God-given purpose? It was a meaningful lesson since we had students who had already lost grandparents or a parent. That serious excursion left us all with heartfelt answers to Mark's questions about mortality.

On several occasions, we spent the entire evening of our home group time reading the Bible. No discussions, we just read scriptures. You could share where you were in your systematic reading of God's Word or pick up suggestions for passages to read from what was on the coffee table. Each random scripture fit together as we rightly divided the Word. We finished each evening filled with truth and a calm frame of mind.

Some nights, all we did was pray when we came together. We prayed scripture, we lifted up nations in prayer, we were quiet and reflected on verses in the Bible, and we prayed for our church staff and the leadership of our great state. We prayed for one another. As they walked out of our home, they left with an overwhelming sense of peace, for we had met with God in an everlasting conversation.

Stations of the cross were set up and ready for each person to enter our home with an admiring attitude of what Christ did for us at Calvary. Scriptures were placed throughout the home where they could take time to pause and reflect on each section of Christ's journey from the garden to the cross.

Our antique wash bowl was filled with warm water, and a sign was taped to the front door. "Take off your shoes; wait until the door opens to come in." As each person entered, Mark and I washed their hands and prayed over them. We handed them scripture and instructed them to go anywhere in the house or outside to read. We asked them to remain there until they heard music and then come to the living room to gather together. As we finished the washing of the hands, we began the washing of the Word as everyone began to read their assigned scriptures. Most evenings, we ended our group with taking home someone's prayer request. We asked that each person spend the next week or two praying for that person and their appeal. Mark asked that they use that written paper request as a bookmark in order to see it every time they opened their Bible.

Everyone enjoyed nights of worship in our home. Some evenings, we had local worship leaders bless us with songs of hope and restoration of our faith. There were also times we played music and sang along with the album. By far, this was one of my favorite gathering times when we worshiped before our great and mighty King. I could have danced all night and continued singing with all my heart. I loved those times before the Lord.

We tried to reserve a jail cell at our local police station for our high school seniors but instead closed the doors of a vacant room at our church. With paper and pen in hand, they were asked to write a letter. If you were considered a modern-day Paul, how would you share the gospel with the person you are writing to? Who did you write your prison letter to, and why?

We headed to a nearby high school on a bright, sunny Sunday. We soon discovered that the football field and track were locked up. The students became excited when they discovered a chair outside the gate just begging for us to use it. Well, yes we did. We jumped over the fence with the assistance of an old metal chair to begin another adventure. Mark and I handed each student a notepad and pen and instructed them to go anywhere in the stadium and write about their lives. They would be graduating from high school soon and heading out into the world, so we thought it would be reflective for them to write down their accomplishments as well as their goals and desires for the future.

We asked if they wanted to read what they wrote to everyone, so here are some of their thoughts on that rule-breaking day.

One girl sat on the track and wrote about her life being likened to a marathon. She knew life was a race and she needed to keep up the pace of putting Christ first. She and her future husband ended up on the mission field for several years, and to this day, they are running hard after the Lord. Several students sat in the stands and wrote about life as a spectator. There were others who wrote sports analogies. One young man sat in the announcer's box and wrote as if he were broadcasting a football game.

I sat on the field right in front of a goalpost. I had accomplished so much in life—marriage, children, serving, teaching, and more. When I completed my thoughts and put my pen down, the Lord spoke to my heart and said, "Turn around." Well, there you have it. The other goalpost far down the field indicated that there was so much more work to be done for the Lord.

No matter where you are in life, I'm here to testify that when you look back on life, you truly see God's hand in everything. It all comes together. Every step along the way, every class, every job, the people you meet, and your neighbors have been given to you as a gift.

It's Acts 17:24–20 coming to fruition.

## To Be Filled by the Holy Spirit

Exodus 31:3, 35:31

Dueteronomy 34:9

Matthew 5:6

Luke 1:15

Luke 1:41

Luke 1:67

Acts 2:2

Acts 2:4

Acts 4:8

Acts 4:31

Acts 9:17

Acts 13:9

Ephesians 5:18

Here are a few more scriptures that educate us on the filling of the Holy Spirit. Enjoy discovering truth as you look up the word *Spirit* in the concordance in your Bible.

# Closing Time

As I write the end of this book, I'm in a government-ordered lockdown due to the coronavirus (COVID-19). How will you look back on this worldwide pandemic of 2020?

This is history in the making, and I am experiencing a full range of emotions. Shelter in place fell during the season of Lent. Today is Palm Sunday, and resurrection Sunday is coming. These are difficult yet exciting times we live in, seeing God at work through this virus outbreak.

We have been instructed to stay in our homes. Most people are working from their places of residence, while others are putting their lives at risk to serve those who are infected with the virus.

People from our neighborhood are out walking every day saying "Hello," "How are you doing?" and "Do you need anything?" We are telling everyone we see in the grocery store and on the street that we are praying for one another and blessing everyone we get within six feet of given our social-distancing requirements.

What I am seeing are large numbers of prayer groups and pictures of beautiful places from around the world shared by those who have had the great privilege to travel abroad in the past. Playing board games and putting together puzzles have become the normal evening pastimes. Deeper conversations are drawing from the well of our souls. Long letters are being written and sent by snail mail. What a delight to read letters of love and support on real paper.

The Bible is being opened and read as many look for the code to unlock secret things for the "end times." The Internet is lit up with pastors preaching and established artists entertaining us for free. We are able to get free movies and workouts, and world-renowned museums are inviting us to visit their art online. The list goes on and on. The numbers are greatly increasing of those listening to Bible-believing teachers and seeking answers from God. Opinions are still being posted, yet I see a great stance of love, truth, and kindness.

It is the same truth we have all been looking for throughout the ages. The answer is profoundly simple: God is in control. God loves you. It is all in the Bible; he told us that this was coming. God desires for us to love and obey him. Why are we so surprised by this?

I'm not ignorant to the evil that is on high alert as well during this time in our world right now. I choose to pray and not give it power by acknowledging it in this book. It's bad, really bad, but where sin abounds, grace abounds much more.

The Lord appeared to Solomon after the temple was built in Jerusalem and said these words:

> *I have heard your prayer and have chosen this place for myself as a temple for sacrifices.*
>
> *When I shut up the heavens so that there is no rain, or command locusts to devour the land or send a plague among my people, if my people, who are called by my name, will humble themselves and pray and seek my face and turn from their wicked ways, then I will hear from heaven, and I will forgive their sin and will heal their land. Now my eyes will be open and my ears attentive to the prayers offered in this place. I have chosen and consecrated this temple so that my Name may be there forever. My eyes and my heart will always be there.*
>
> —2 Chron. 7:12–16

I'm not saying it's the end of the world as we know it, yet I do believe the church must repent. What God has established from the get-go is for his people to choose life. Remember, God is calling all people to repent everywhere.

But I feel that the greatest destroyer of peace today is abortion, because it is a war against the child, a direct killing of the innocent child, murder by the mother herself. And if we accept that a mother can kill even her own child, how can we tell other people not to kill one another? How do we persuade a woman not to have an abortion? As always, we must persuade her with love and we remind ourselves that love means to be willing to give until it hurts. Jesus gave even His life to love us. So, the mother who is thinking of abortion, should be helped to love, that is, to give until it hurts her plans, or her free time, to respect the life of her child. The father of that child, whoever he is, must also give until it hurts.[1]

How do you respond to these words written by this fearless saint?

The church must fall on its face and cry out, "Forgive us, Lord, for sinning against you and you alone." You see, when God asked the Israelites to take out a people group (and there were so many), it was due to their despicable sins in the eyes of God. The word *despicable* means deserving hatred and contempt. The very reason God asked the Israelites to take out people groups in the Old Testament was because they had done evil in the sight of the Lord. They were sacrificing babies to their gods and ignoring the one true God. If you pull up the worldwide deaths this year on the worldometer website (https://www.worldometers.info/), you will see that abortion is in the lead for the top 11 rated deaths in the world.

Oh, how this grieves me to know that people groups in the Old Testament would sacrifice their children, swap partners, burn disabled children, and, well, the list goes on and on and on. Are we any different today? I'm not pushing any political agenda, just calling it as I see it. "Chose life," God said.

To this day, God desires a people to be called out, to be holy as God is holy. He also knew we would fail, so he gave us his only Son to die for our sins. Jesus overcame sin and darkness and conquered the grave. He

---

1. Mother Theresa, "Blessed Mother Teresa on Abortion," Speech at the National Prayer Breakfast, Washington, DC, February 5, 1994, https://www.catholicnewsagency.com/resources/abortion/catholic-teaching/blessed-mother-teresa-on-abortion.

rose again and will soon conquer the enemy that is filled with pride and arrogance. The Spirit and the bride say, "Come."

Please hear my heart. I, too, have been changed by stories of abortion, and there is no judgment here. My story is one of grace, forgiveness, and love. I'm grateful that God redeemed me. He has redeemed you, too.

As I am praying now, I'm weeping, lamenting. Such sorrow and grief mingled together.

It is both joy and sorrow that fill these bones, my mind, and my heart.

My insides are torn apart with the devastation and grief associated with loss and death.

I'm praying for the homeless, abused children, women, and men. I'm lifting up single parents before you, God. Please provide for those who live paycheck to paycheck. May others come alongside to assist those in need.

I boldly ask you, God, to sing over those who are alone or living in a nursing home. Sing over this world, and cover us with your amazing love, grace, and protection. Just as you covered the earth and called it into existence, hover over us now, Lord, and allow us to know that you are near to the brokenhearted. There are so many on the front lines who are willing to lay down their own lives to save another's.

Thank you, nurses, doctors, and hospital staff. Thank you, police officers, firefighters, and paramedics. Thank you to all those who are working behind the scenes to stock our stores with food and supplies. We are living with grateful hearts.

My soul weeps, and my mind races. Yet I remember . . . I recall that you are sovereign and in control of all things.

Now, assurance is beginning to fill my heart. In the midst of the chaos, there is hope.

The church is starting to wake up from her deep slumber. Oh, may we repent and turn our faces back to a holy God.

On that glorious day when we will lay our crowns down at God's feet and understand with immeasurable faith that:

Jesus is King!
Resurrection Sunday is coming!
Who do you know who needs prayer?
How will you pray?

What will you pray?

When will you pray?

Where will you pray?

Who are you praying for?

Lord, I pray for pastors who are continuing to shepherd with the truth of the gospel. Embolden us with your powerful Holy Spirit to talk about the Way to everyone.

Help us remember that we are all the same at the foot of the cross. We are all made in your beautiful image, the Imago Dei.

Thank you, brothers and sisters of all nationalities who have been martyred for your faith for centuries, for your undying beliefs in the one true God, Yahweh.

This is Christ's love being displayed throughout the world. We can follow the example set before us as Christ laid down his life for all people.

Come, Holy Spirit, come. Let us truly understand that the Word of God is active and alive, sharper than any two-edged sword. The Word is alive; it will not return void. Holy Spirit, empower us so we can lift up your name, proclaim your love, and care for our family, our neighbors, and our nation.

God, you alone will receive all the glory and power and praise forevermore.

And when we stand before God, we will hear, "Well done, good and faithful servant!" (Matt. 25:23).

Heed these words. Indeed, your everlasting conversations are being stored up before the Lord with the smoke of incense along with prayers of the saints, past, present, and future. An angel will take those tear-filled prayers and place them on the golden altar and then hurl them out upon the earth. Those prayers will pour out in order for salvation to come to the lost in Jesus's name (Rev. 8:3–5).

On all occasions, keep on praying, saints.

> Prayer is the most wonderful act in the spiritual realm as well as the most mysterious affair.[2]

---

2. Watchman Nee, *Spiritual Authority* (New York: Christian Fellowship Publishers, 1972), Google Books.

# Acknowledgments

Rachael Rosser, thank you for asking me to go and serve in Africa. Thank you for encouraging me to write a book on prayer. You are truly a loyal friend and soul daughter to Mark and me.

Steve and Julie Hardin, your evangelistic heart spurs everyone to tell others of the good news of Jesus Christ. If you live in Texas, you know Steve Hardin and his love for Jesus. I remember after he preached one time, I leaned over to my daughter and said, "We get to know Steve Hardin!" He's the real deal y'all.

Dick and Cindy Read, thank you for inviting us to student ministry. Your smiles, laughter, and deep love for teaching the Word of God shaped and matured us. You are family to us.

Matt Chandler, your insatiable passion to preach the Word of God and live out that truth is inspiring. Your wit and honest approach to life can stir an auditorium to deeper faith due to your personal crisis of faith. Thank you for leadership in the Acts 29 ministry. You and Lauren have so many gifts, and prayer is at the top of that long list.

Keith Wheeler, you answered the call to go, and the world has witnessed a man and the cross. Life's addresses have been changed due to your obedience. Your smile and love for people is inspirational.

Rachel Joy, how you love the Lord and encourage women to be in the Word and love one another.

Kyle Worley, pastor, friend, and adopted son, your brilliant mind and humble heart continue to lead the city of Richardson, Texas, one step closer to the one true relationship with Jesus. For you and your elders to graciously bring communion to every member on Easter during the shelter in place of 2020 reveals your compassion for your flock. You have a shepherd's heart for people to know the way, the truth, and the life in Christ.

Isaac Munji, Esther, and family, you have taken adversity and turned it into grace for the people of Nakuru. God raised you up through your pain to help the abused and abandoned have hope. Your and Esther's heart for the low-born women of Kenya is for them to be seen and valued.

Thanks to the author of a worldwide prayer ministry who inspired me years ago to rewrite the next chapter on prayer. Your little drawing of yourself with two fingers making the peace sign was a prophetic statement. Thanks for inspiring me through your books on prayer. I hope this is a good addition.

# About the Author

Jana Hoffman is an evangelist, teacher, and encourager who is humbled to come alongside others in prayer. She has a heart for missions and has participated in short-term mission trips to Mexico, Guatemala, Estonia, Jamaica, Africa, and several large US cities. And she loves to hike 14ers—actually, any mountain.

Jana has been involved in many ministries, including the following:

- Student lay leader for 18 years in Tulsa, Oklahoma, at Asbury United Methodist Church
- Kay Arthur Precept Ministries for 15 years, taking classes, training, and teaching inductive Bible studies
- Moms in Touch International, praying for her children in the schools they attended for 12 years
- Perspectives, 18-week World Missions College Credit Training
- Association of Biblical Counseling certification, Dallas, Texas
- Biblical counseling ministry, www.hoffmanbiblicalcounseling.com
- The Institute Training Program at The Village Church, Dallas, Texas
- Association of Biblical Counseling teacher and counselor in Zambia for two years
- Trauma training and counseling, Kenya, Africa, for two years
- Strategic Ministries, a three-year Bible study on the Holy Spirit, Houston, Texas, www.strategicministries.com
- On staff at The Village Church, Dallas, Texas, for two years
- Deacon of prayer at several churches in Oklahoma and Texas
- Bible study teacher, premarital counselor, home group leader, and mentor to younger generations
- Steps program and mentor at The Village Church, Dallas, Texas
- Biblical counselor in a South Dallas school
- Paraprofessional at a charter high school

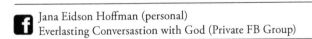 Jana Eidson Hoffman (personal)
Everlasting Conversastion with God (Private FB Group)

 @jana_hoffman
Jana Hoffman

# TAG

*The LORD confides in those who fear him; he makes his covenant known to them.*

—Ps. 25:14

Choose a name of God, one of his attributes, or a character of God. Look up the related scriptures, read them, and pray them. Ask God to speak directly to you.

> *Open my eyes that I may see*
> *wonderful things in your law.*

—Ps. 119:18

Date _____ Attribute _____

Definition _____

Scripture _____

_____

What does this mean to you personally? _____

Ask God, "How does this apply to me, Lord?"_____

Write a prayer thanking God for the specific thoughts he has impressed upon you today.

**Write out your prayer requests for today:**

_____

_____

_____

_____

_____

_____

_____

_____

_____

_____

_____

_____

_____

_____

_____

# Recommendations of Books and Websites about Prayer

The Bible by God

*Lord, Teach Me to Pray* by Kay Arthur

*Practicing the Power* by Sam Storms

*Enthroned* by David Fritch

*Prayer, Conversing with God* by Rosalind Rinker

*Intercessory Prayer* by Dutch Sheets

*The Singing God* by Sam Storms

*Red Moon Rising* by Pete Greig and Dave Roberts

*The Holy Spirit & You* by Dennis & Rita Bennett

*Let Us Pray* by Watchman Nee

*Spiritual Authority* by Watchman Nee

*The Release of the Spirit* by Watchman Nee

*Experiencing God* by Henry & Richard Blackaby and Claude King

*Lord, I Want to Know You* by Kay Arthur

*They Speak with Other Tongues* by John Sherrill

*The Book of Common Prayer* by the Church of England

Moms in Prayer International, www.momsinprayer.org

Precept, www.precept.org

Strategic Ministries Inc., www.strategicministries.com

CPSIA information can be obtained
at www.ICGtesting.com
Printed in the USA
LVHW082039041220
673103LV00005B/338